HIDDEN HISTORY *of* LAKE ERIE

Jennifer Boresz Engelking

Published by The History Press
An imprint of Arcadia Publishing
Charleston, SC
www.historypress.com

First published 2025

Manufactured in the United States

ISBN 9781467159678

Library of Congress Control Number: 2025943122

To my husband, Brian.

Thank you for always believing in me, loving me

and watching Lake Erie sunsets with me.

Happy fifteenth anniversary!

I love you.

Contents

Rolling waves on Lake Erie. *Photo by author.*

Preface

There's something about watching the rhythmic waves in Lake Erie that is mesmerizing, like staring at the flickering flames in a bonfire. It's both calming and inspiring, and I find my thoughts drifting to the stories I've heard over the years growing up near the lake, wondering which parts are legend and which are fact. What lies below the surface? Is there some truth to the many Lake Erie Monster sightings? Did people see a log floating on the water or a long fish or eel? What about the hundreds of Lake Erie shipwrecks and treasures that some are said to hold? Are gold coins really scattered across the lake floor, waiting to be found?

I wrote this book to try to answer those questions and I did in fact find the answers to many, but other stories still have gaps—newspaper reports that are missing or inconsistencies in storytellers' versions of an event—which I think adds to the intrigue of Lake Erie.

This is not a complete history of Lake Erie or the region surrounding it because there are other wonderful books that cover those details. *Hidden History of Lake Erie* contains a variety of little-known stories about interesting characters, places and events from Lake Erie's islands and along its shores. One recent discovery took my breath away, and I'm honored to write about it and include it in the last pages of this book. I've lived along Lake Erie's shores all my life, and through my research and writing, I have gained a new appreciation for our small but mighty lake and the people who have called it home. And after reading this, I hope you will too.

Acknowledgements

When I was a little girl, I dreamed of being an author, and I am so thankful for the opportunity to write four books in the past six years! Thank you to The History Press/Arcadia Publishing for helping make my dream come true. Special thanks to my commissioning editor, Joe Gartrell, and copy editor, Ashley Hill!

Thank you to the wonderful people I interviewed who shared their stories and photos with me—you are the heart of my book. A big thanks to scuba diver Mark Lasmanis for allowing me to share the story of his incredible underwater discoveries. Thank you to the archivists at various libraries and historical societies who helped me track down fascinating images and information.

Thank you to the owners of the many stores and small businesses who sell my books—I am so grateful for you!

A huge thank-you to you, dear reader. Your kind words and encouragement mean so much to me and motivate me to keep writing!

Thank you to my incredible family and friends. I am blessed to be surrounded by so much love and support. Thank you to my wonderful Mom and Dad, Joanne and Dale Boresz—I am so thankful to be your daughter. I cherish the time you spent reading to me as a kid, giving me the foundation for a lifelong love of stories, and our fun visits to the beach gave me a true appreciation for the lake. Thank you for everything and for always believing in me, which gave me the confidence to believe in myself and go after my dreams, like becoming an author. (And thank you, Dad, for all of your help with my website and for proofreading!)

Thank you to my Mother-in-Law and Father-in-Law, Mary Ann and Dave Engelking. You've been an important part of my life for more than two decades, and I am thankful for how you've always embraced me into your family since those early days and for how supportive you have been of me since then. When it comes to parents and grandparents for our kids, Brian and I really hit the jackpot with you four! We love you!

Thank you to my handsome husband, Brian. You always make me feel special, make me laugh and cheer me on! Thank you for letting me bounce story ideas off you, for making deliveries to restock my books, for helping at signings and for always listening to my *many* future book ideas. I'm glad you yelled out, "I love you, Jen!" as you walked past my writing class at Cleveland State twenty-some years ago. It was one of the moments that started an incredible adventure with you, and I am so thankful for every second of it!

And thank you to our three wonderful children, our "little birdies," who are growing up so fast. It is my greatest joy and honor in life to be your mom. I am thankful to God for each of you—to watch each milestone as you grow and to go on adventures, big and small, with you. Thank you for always being proud of me and for helping me hit the "send" button each time I finish a book manuscript. Thank you for always making me laugh, for your hugs and for reminding me that the greatest joy in life is found in the little moments we share together. I will always love you with all my heart and soul, and I will always be proud of you.

Opposite: Map of Lake Erie. *Designed by Andrew McManus.*

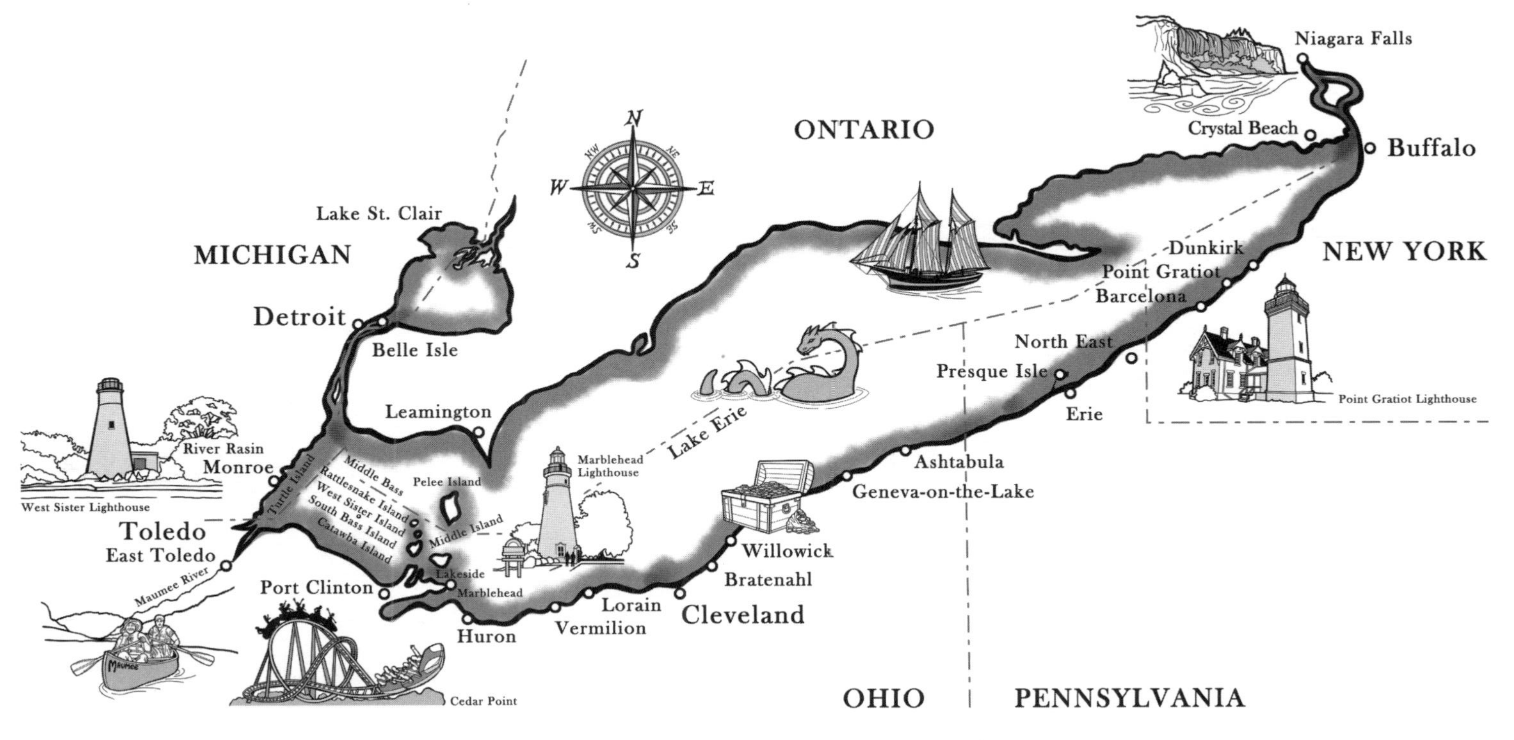

Niagara Falls
Crystal Beach
Buffalo
ONTARIO
NEW YORK
Dunkirk
Point Gratiot
Barcelona
North East
Presque Isle
Erie
Point Gratiot Lighthouse
Lake St. Clair
MICHIGAN
Detroit
Belle Isle
Leamington
Lake Erie
Marblehead Lighthouse
Ashtabula
Geneva-on-the-Lake
Willowick
Bratenahl
Cleveland
Lorain
Vermilion
Huron
River Rasin
Monroe
West Sister Lighthouse
Turtle Island
Middle Bass
Rattlesnake Island
West Sister Island
South Bass Island
Catawba Island
Pelee Island
Middle Island
Lakeside
Marblehead
Toledo
East Toledo
Maumee River
Port Clinton
Cedar Point
OHIO
PENNSYLVANIA

I

Industries and Transportation

Lake Erie has long been a bustling waterway. People and goods have traveled across its quickly changing waters for centuries. It's the fourth largest of the Great Lakes by surface area, but it is the shallowest, averaging a depth of just sixty-two-feet, and is the smallest by volume. This geographic combination allows the lake to go from having a calm, glass-like surface to treacherous waves in a matter of minutes.

It was created thousands of years ago when it was carved out by glaciers. Water enters Lake Erie via the Detroit River from the upper Great Lakes and Lake St. Clair and empties into the Niagara River, where it careens over the falls and into Lake Ontario.

The fertile land and unique lakefront ecosystem drew Natives as the region's earliest inhabitants. These Natives included the Erie, for whom the lake is named.

The cities and towns that dot the lake's coast, from Detroit, Michigan, in the west to Buffalo, New York, in the east, have played major roles in the lake's history. Industries developed, tragedies occurred and legends were born.

Above: A midsummer blue-sky view of Lake Erie. *Photo by author.*

Opposite: River Raisin Massacre Monument, Monroe, Michigan, 1940s. *Author's collection.*

Monroe: Piers, Paradise and Port

A Battle

Monroe, Michigan, is a small town steeped in history. It sits on the western end of Lake Erie, between Detroit, Michigan, and Toledo, Ohio, where the River Raisin National Battlefield Park marks the site of the largest battle fought on Michigan soil. The Battle of Frenchtown occurred over several days in January 1813.

The confrontation began when Americans forced the British and Natives to retreat from Frenchtown (Monroe), which they occupied. The United States hoped this would help its troops advance north to retake Fort Detroit after its loss the previous summer. Although the Americans believed they were successful, the British and Natives, led by Tecumseh, a Shawnee chief and warrior who resisted the expansion of the United States into Native lands, launched a counterattack several days later.

Because the Americans weren't prepared, it was a great victory for the British and Native confederation and one of the bloodiest engagements during the War of 1812, according to the River Raisin Battlefield website. The battle's aftermath led to laws that forced the removal, relocation and assimilation of Native nations in the United States, according to the National Park Service.

The Piers

Alongside the memory of this brutal battle existed great beauty that lured wildlife and visitors.

"By 1905, an estimated 70,000 people were visiting Lake Erie at the River Raisin's mouth each summer, drawn by the Monroe Piers Resort Park which included a light house, casino and dancing pavilion, swimming beach, commercial roller coaster, carousel and small luxury hotel, the Hotel Lotus," according to an article by David L. Eby in the *Monroe News*.

To meet the demand, the bathhouse was enlarged to two stories with three hundred changing rooms, which included a bathing suit, towel and a locker for a twenty-five-cent rental fee, according to the Historical Marker Database. A historical marker at the site described a seventy-five-foot-tall roller coaster that was added in 1905, when electricity was installed; it was crowned by a circle of one thousand incandescent lights.

Weekend regattas became a tradition as Lotus Hotel guests and sailors competed on the waterfront. Around the same time, the Monroe Yacht Club was built on the south pier and quickly became part of the Lake Erie sailing scene.

"Regattas were an event for the ladies to wear their finest summer dresses and for the men to proudly display their 'yachting uniform.' Competition between the Monroe and Toledo clubs was keen," the plaque reads. "In 1905, a large entertainment building was built on the north pier. Called 'The Casino,' it offered refreshments on the first floor and a dance hall on the second. The Yacht Club purchased the financially struggling enterprise in 1916 and, after making several improvements that included the addition of double porches on all sides, moved into its new clubhouse."

One of the club's most prominent social events was its annual muskrat dinner, held each December. In 1905, 1,800 guests feasted on the unique entrée of local muskrat, making national headlines.

"Social dignitaries from as far as Seattle and New York came to dine at the annual affair. One year, Commodore Sterling created a large replica of a muskrat house in the center of the ballroom, complete with stuffed 'rats' and glass to simulate ice. Sterling wanted each guest to understand what a marsh rat was," according to the Historical Marker Database.

The popularity of the piers dwindled by the 1920s, due to the development of the highways that allowed vacationers to travel to farther destinations.

Hotel Lotus at Monroe Piers, 1908. *Author's collection.*

Sailboats "just before the race" at Monroe Piers, 1909. *Author's collection.*

Johnson's Island

Idyllic islands, including Johnson's Island, dotted the water near Monroe. (The name, Johnson's Island, is also shared by another Lake Erie island located near Port Clinton, Ohio, which had a Civil War Confederate POW camp and cemetery on it. Its history is included in my book *Lost Lake Erie*.)

Johnson's Island, located near Monroe, was a beautiful summer resort at the turn of the twentieth century. It was named after Detroit business executive Benjamin Johnson, who bought the island in 1891 with plans to develop it into a summer retreat for himself, his wife and her sister.

According to Eby's *Monroe News* article, they moved to the island several years later, raised cattle and fruit and planted beautiful gardens that included lilac paths, flowering shrubs and arbors. Johnson built a baseball park and grandstand, a boat dock and summer cottages and opened his home as a private resort, where guests could feast on game and fish from the lake marsh and vegetables from his garden.

The popularity of the resort began to wane around the same time as the Monroe Piers, and it became hard for Johnson to keep up with his financial responsibilities. He decided to give up his paradise and took a job as manager at the Hotel Lotus, but soon after, while serving guests, his heart failed at the age of fifty-nine. Many believed his decision to give up his home led to his untimely death. Johnson's widow and her sister moved to the mainland afterward, and the island soon fell into disrepair.

A postcard of Lily Pond on Johnson's Island, Monroe, Michigan, 1908. It reads, "145-degrees in the shade. Were [*sic*] using bed sheets to keep prespiration [*sic*] off. Papa and Florine." *Author's collection.*

Then in 1929, the property was bought by the Newton Steel Co., which brought more than one thousand jobs to the region. However, according to David L. Eby, the island was absorbed by the construction of the plant. Through the following decades, the factory and property would have different owners, including companies like Republic Steel and Ford.

The Port

Monroe was also becoming an important Lake Erie port.

During the immigration boom in the mid-1800s, as European immigrants traveled across the ocean and through the Great Lakes, people poured through Monroe at LaPlaisance Bay. It was a bustling spot and the only port on the western end of Lake Erie, according to the Port of Monroe website. From the 1920s through the '40s, the Port of Monroe was established, the harbor and canal were dredged and a dock, terminal building and gantry cranes were installed along the turning basin to handle the processing of packaged, baled and bagged freight.

In the 1960s, the port became a pivotal spot for Lake Erie industry, storing ten thousand Renault cars per year bound for international markets, along with Pittsburgh steamship fleet vessels during the winter.

A 1968 advertisement that can be found on the Port of Monroe's website boasts Monroe was "Michigan's only port on Lake Erie and the largest manufacturing center for paper shipping containers and folding paper boxes."

By the 1970s, a power plant was built that became one of the largest energy-generating plants in Michigan, and the Boblo boats, headed to and from Boblo Island (a popular amusement park), made round trips from the Port of Monroe.

Industry in Monroe has continued to grow over the years, which is great for the economy but not the natural habitats of the River Raisin and Lake Erie.

"The cost of doing business in the midst of this transformation resulted in some chronic pollution problems, including PCBs in river sediments and an on-going need to dredge the lower channel for ship traffic," reads Monroe's website. "In the 1930s, as a Works Progress Administration (WPA) project, a series of dams were constructed to carry sanitary sewer across the River Raisin's bedrock bottom. But the dams have blocked boats and fish from travelling back up the Raisin from Lake Erie."

To combat this, the Environmental Protection Agency, Michigan Department of Environmental Quality and River Raisin Public Advisor Council developed a remedial action plan, investing millions of dollars to enhance the recreational and environmental potential in the River Raisin and nearby Sterling State Park, including removing some of the dams to allow fish and small boats to pass through.

It is transforming the region into a peaceful refuge once again.

BRATENAHL'S STREET LAMPLIGHTER

The *clip clop* of horses' hooves and the distant rumble of a wooden cart could be heard on the hard-packed clay streets.

As the sound came closer, the ethereal glow of streetlamps could be seen popping up slowly, like fireflies at twilight, at first faint and then brighter as the lamplighter neared.

Colonel Aaron Williams made his way through the Village of Bratenahl each night and early morning to light and extinguish the gas streetlamps on the unpaved, tree-lined streets and some estate driveways.

He was a familiar sight in his green two-wheel lamp cart, "Lamplighter" printed on the back and drawn by his horse Molly, with his reins in one hand and an old-fashioned gasoline flare in the other.

According to the Bratenahl Historical Society, Williams was "a red-cheeked, ever-cheerful, warm-hearted lighter of lamps. He was a village character, a sort of unofficial town crier. No matter what the weather, he was on the job, always cheery in returning greetings. The children who followed him on his rounds called him Santa Claus for his long white hair and beard. They were amazed that he never ignited his beard with the flame from the naphtha torches he carried from lamp to lamp."

He was an old Indian Scout, said to work with Buffalo Bill, who came to the village in 1898 at around fifty years old from Bay City, Michigan. He quickly became friends with the villagers and knew everyone by name.

He first began lighting lamps in what was known as Glenville on the Lake, with fifty lamps to care for and a payment of a dollar per lamp.

"In 1905, a resolution was presented to the council declaring it necessary to light all streets within the Village," reads the Village of Bratenahl's website. "Lake Shore Boulevard was unpaved and arched by tall oaks, sycamores, and elms. Side streets were lanes. Council signed a contract with Canton,

Aaron Williams, Bratenahl's gaslamp lighter. *Courtesy of the Bratenahl Historical Society.*

Ohio's Sun Vapor Light Company, to furnish and maintain not less than 121 gas Weisbach Street Lights."

That number increased to two hundred, placed 150 feet apart throughout the village.

"Molly knew every lamp along the boulevard. She crisscrossed without a 'giddap' or 'whoa.' Aaron was so fond of Molly that when it came time to replace her, he said, 'I wouldn't part with her for the world, not even if all the folks out there chipped in and bought me a $5,000 machine. Molly deserves a good rest in her old age, and she's going to have it," according to the Village of Bratenahl's site.

Eventually, Molly was replaced by a Model T Ford, but it was never as efficient, since Molly had been going about her route each day for so long.

According to the Village of Bratenahl's site, "Williams reflected, 'Tending lamps isn't such a monotonous occupation as it sounds. I've narrowly escaped death several times in runaways and automobile crashes.' But even while recovering from injuries received in these accidents, Williams was faithful to his trust and never missed more than two or three days at best."

Williams rode from lamppost to lamppost for twenty-four years, retiring in his seventies in 1922. He then parked his Model T in a place of honor in his yard.

Williams died seven years later at the age of eighty-two. Two decades later, lighting engineers determined the amount of illumination provided by the old gas lamps wasn't enough to even register on a light meter at pavement level, so the village announced that 153 of the gas streetlights that had glowed throughout Bratenahl since 1905 would be replaced by 123 electric streetlights.

The gas lights, owned by the Weisbach Gas Mantle Co. of Philadelphia, were sent to that bustling Pennsylvania city because it still used gas lights.

And so ended an era in this stretch along Lake Erie—the soft glow of flickering gas lights died, and the dawn of electricity began.

The Cleveland Golf Club

At the height of the Gilded Age, the successful businessmen behind the most profitable downtown Cleveland industries owned mansions on Cleveland's Millionaires' Row. They spent their workdays amid the smog and grime of the city and enjoyed escaping to the clean air of the country.

In 1889, a small, informal group of horseback riders in the Bit & Bridle Club, who enjoyed riding from their Cleveland mansions to the countryside along Lake Erie, began imagining the construction of a log cabin–style clubhouse near Dugway Brook to extend their weekly horseback excursions, according to the Village of Bratenahl's site.

As word spread among the Cleveland elite, the interest was so great that the club instead decided to create an elaborate lakefront social club at 11409 Lakeshore Boulevard that became known as The Country Club of Cleveland, with membership limited to one hundred.

The club bought fifteen acres of land on Eddy Road from Charles Coit, who, at one point, owned a tract of eighty acres and owned a local hotel, according to the Village of Bratenahl's site.

Cleveland industrialist Samuel Mather, partner at Pickands Mather & Company, was the club president, and once, while on a business trip,

The Country Club in Bratenahl, 1889–99. *Courtesy of the Bratenahl Historical Society.*

Golfers believed to be in front of the first clubhouse, early 1890s. *Courtesy of the Bratenahl Historical Society.*

he played golf at the Saint Andrew's Golf Club in Hastings-on-Hudson, New York, and returned with a passion for this new game. As a result, he organized the Cleveland Golf Club, a subsidiary of The Country Club. Officers were elected, with Mather leading as the president, and only members of The Country Club could join.

The club leased grounds from Charles Coit for links east of Eddy Road, with stipulations that the club provide a fence to keep out the cows. A nine-hole course was built north of the boulevard, along with a pro shop and caddy shack. It opened on July 13, 1895, the first golf course west of the Appalachian Mountains. Members began referring to golf as "pasture pool," and it became an integral part of club activities for men and women.

According to the Village of Bratenahl's site, the *Cleveland Leader* reported:

> *The course of the club begins near the lake, and the first hazard is a six-foot hedge, a wire fence, and a bunker, on top of which is a huge, varicolored Japanese parasol shading a rustic bench. The course runs south to the railroad track, west to Eddy Road, and then north again on the west side of the green to the finishing hole near the lake.*

Mather convinced professional golfer Joe Mitchell to come to Bratenahl as the club's first professional. However, his arrival was met without fanfare as he carried his bag of clubs up a dusty road from the Coit station to the club, where he found a three-room shack without running water. According to the Great Cleveland Sports Hall of Fame, Mitchell collaborated with Cleveland businessman and sportsman Coburn Haskell to invent the rubber-cored, rubber-wound golf ball, still used in its modified form.

The clubhouse was unfortunately destroyed by fire on October 1, 1899, when the fireplace's hearth, built on heavy floor joists, burst into flames. A new, larger clubhouse was built on Coit Road, farther back from the lake, and additional sporting facilities were added, including swimming pools and croquet courses.

A rift among golfers and non-golfing members, whose opinions differed on whether it was primarily a social club or a golf club, pushed Cleveland Golf Club members to acquire a clubhouse of their own. They bought and remodeled a country home on Coit Road, added a restaurant and opened the clubhouse on May 5, 1900. To manage the expansive lawn, they decided to buy a flock of sheep, which was less expensive than hiring men to mow and more picturesque.

Joe Mitchell, 1919. *Courtesy of the Bratenahl Historical Society.*

In 1900, the *Plain Dealer* described the new Cleveland Golf Club:

> *The house was a quaint rambling structure standing in a grove of trees only a step away from the Shoreline cars. There were about twelve acres around the house with plenty of trees, pretty walks, a rustic summer home, and a most romantic bridge spanning a little gully which at one time accommodated a little stream but has only grasses, ferns, and wildflowers.*

Club members could watch the links while lounging on a broad veranda or head inside to enjoy the lounging and dining rooms and women's and men's locker rooms. However, the Cleveland Golf Club's separate accommodations were short-lived, because by 1902, they consolidated again with The Country Club and returned to its recently built clubhouse.

A few years later, the second clubhouse was destroyed in a fire, but members set up tents on the lawn so social activities could continue. A third clubhouse, designed by Abram Garfield (the son of President James Garfield, who had lived east of the club in Mentor) was completed in 1908. It was even more magnificent, featuring a ballroom, library and glass-enclosed lake-view dining room.

"Above the bar and grill was a large veranda where summer tea dances were held, and breathtaking sunsets were enjoyed," reads the Village of Bratenahl's site.

The golf course grew to include eighteen holes and was the site of the first airplane flight in Cleveland. According to Paul Soprano on AviationCLE.com, the flight took place on June 28, 1910, with a French-built Demoiselle monoplane owned by a group of Cleveland investors.

At 7:30 p.m., Captain William A. Mattery cranked the gasoline engine of his airplane, which had a wingspan of twenty-five feet and was about the same length, and then climbed in between the uprights and rose into the air. The plane's wings were made of yellow silk, stitched tight on a hollow metal frame, and slender wires adjusted the wings and tail. Mattery circled The Country Club's golf links twice at a height varying between five to ten feet, and when an essential wire grew slack, Mattery shut off the engine and landed the plane smoothly on the ground.

About two hundred people gathered on the golf course to watch the unannounced flight (at the present location of the Haskell Homes of Newport, named after the inventor of the modern golf ball).

The Country Club was in its prime for nearly two decades, but by 1926, the once-quiet stretch of land was becoming surrounded by industry.

"The noise and aroma of halted livestock trains negatively impacted the adjacent golfers," reads the Village of Bratenahl's site. "Factory workers eating their lunches along the perimeter of the course were audibly appreciative of the female players. However, gentlemen golfers were treated with disruptive taunts from industrial onlookers, 'Hit it, Percy, hit it!'"

In 1928, the Van Sweringen brothers, who developed Shaker Heights, proposed the club build a new clubhouse in Pepper Pike on a large parcel of land on Lander Road (where The Country Club still exists).

The former site became known as Lake Shore Country Club and was threatened by encroaching industrial buildings and a newly anticipated highway. In 1942, it reopened as a nine-hole public course, but several years later, George Young and Edward Flannigan, who owned the Roxy burlesque theater in Cleveland, bought the club, investing $150,000 into constructing a bathing beach and glass-enclosed lakeside dining room. When Flannigan died in 1964, Young sold the property to the Bratenahl Development Corporation, and the clubhouse was razed to make room for Bratenahl Place, the first high-rise condominium building in Ohio.

Naming a Ship

In the early twentieth century, steamships plied the waters of the Great Lakes, carrying passengers and cargo from port to port.

Many steamships were named after Great Lakes cities, like *City of Detroit*, *City of Buffalo*, *City of Erie* and *City of Cleveland.* But how did they get their names?

According to the Naval History and Heritage Command website, during the Civil War, the navy expanded quickly, and hundreds of ships were built and bought for naval use.

"Ironclads, including monitors, and shallow-draft river steamers, fell into new classification categories, and their naming reflected the abrupt pace of growth," says the Navy History and Heritage Command website. "Names like *Hartford and Brooklyn*, *Ticonderoga* and *Monongahela* mingled with *Trefoil*, *Stars and Stripes*, *Penguin*, and *Western World*."

Many ships, including gunboats and monitors (small warships), were given Native names. Eventually, it was decided that state names would be used for battleships, but by the early 1900s, they began to run out.

"Monitors and armored cruisers were renamed for cities within their respective name states to free the names of their states for assignment to new battleships," reads the Navy History and Heritage Command website. "The monitors *Florida* and *Nevada*, for example, became *Tallahassee* and *Tonopah*."

City of Buffalo steamship, August 5, 1909. *Author's collection.*

Left: *City of Cleveland* postcard, August 6, 1910. *Courtesy of Allen John Kowalcyk.*

Below: The lobby and grand stairway, *City of Cleveland* postcard. *Courtesy of Allen John Kowalcyk.*

The *City of Cleveland* was part of the legendary Detroit & Cleveland Navigation Company (D&C). It was considered one of the finest passenger liners to ever sail the Great Lakes, but it was also one of the more unfortunate liners.

A fire during the ship's construction in May 1907 delayed its scheduled June debut. "The vessel's elaborate interior woodwork and fittings were nearly finished at the time. Despite two fireboats and onshore firefighting equipment, the only things that could be salvaged were her hull and machinery. Damage was calculated at about $700,000," according to Historic Detroit. "'The fire broke out just before daylight in some mysterious manner. There are rumors afloat that an incendiary is suspected,' the *Mansfield* (Ohio) *News* reported the day of the fire. 'The officials of the shipyard are at a loss to explain the fire, as there were two watchmen on the ship and another at the gate of the shipyard.'"

The 402-foot-long steamship cost $1.25 million to rebuild, and it ushered in a new age of elegance, with custom-designed chandeliers and luxury furnishings. It made its maiden voyage in June 1908. Its name was changed to *City of Cleveland III* in 1912. Decades later in 1950, when the steamship business was dwindling due to the rise of airplane travel and the construction of the interstate, the *City of Cleveland III* once again met a destructive and tragic fate. It was carrying eighty-nine passengers on a cruise to Detroit when a speeding freighter crashed into its side, killing four passengers. It then sat, waiting to be repaired, at a Detroit dock for several years when it came loose from its moorings during a storm and ran aground at Hennepin Point. After later catching on fire and partially sinking, the *City of Cleveland III* was sold for scrap and sent to Buffalo, New York, in 1956.

"A fate that also met her four remaining sister ships of the D&C fleet that same year," according to Historic Detroit.

And the era of naming and christening the palace steamers that once cruised so grandly across Lake Erie came to an end.

GOTHIC ROOM: *CITY OF DETROIT III*

Imagine the grandeur of boarding a Lake Erie steamship in the early twentieth century.

It must have been thrilling—albeit nerve-wracking, since steamships didn't have the best safety record—to see the sheer size of the ship and the opulent detail inside.

City of Detroit III was one of the lake's infamous steamships. It was the sister ship of *City of Cleveland III*, and both were owned and operated by the D&C Lake Line.

A 1923 catalogue from the line, accessible through the Detroit Historical Society, called them "two great giants of the Great Lakes" and described the experience aboard:

> *Night-time and moonlight—the balm of summer air—a glorious open deck—a cigar—a few friends or your family—what could be more comfortable or enjoyable? And you arrive the next day refreshed.*

Above: *City of Detroit III* steamship, 1918. *Author's collection.*

Opposite, top: The Gothic Room aboard *City of Detroit III*, 1912. *Library of Congress.*

Opposite, bottom: LaSalle Window in the Gothic Room, *City of Detroit III*, 1912. *Library of Congress.*

> *Because the D. and C. is essentially a commercial and tourist route for the first-class traveling public making pleasant trips between the great cities on Lake Erie—between Detroit and Buffalo, and Detroit and Cleveland—you will always find plenty of room on deck.*

In 1911, D&C commissioned the famous ship designer Frank E. Kirby to build "the largest steel-hulled passenger side-wheeler on the Great Lakes," according to Dan Austin of the Detroit Historical Society.

City of Detroit III, considered Kirby's crowning achievement, was the most expensive, largest and most luxurious passenger freshwater vessel afloat at the time.

More than six thousand people, including Kirby and D&C officials, came to see *City of Detroit III* launched at the Wyandotte, Michigan yard of the Detroit Shipbuilding Company on October 7, 1911, according to Historic Detroit.

The *Detroit Free Press* provided the play-by-play: "Tense silence, the scarcely audible thump of a sharp-bladed ax biting through hempen bonds, a creaking of timbers, the splintering crackle of breaking glass, then an ear-

FRENCH
LED by LA SALLE
DISCOVER

filling, nerve-jarring volume of sound, ending in a mighty crash as the water displaced by the great mass of steel swept the opposite side of the slip."

While Kirby designed the ship and its exterior, Louis O. Keil designed its interior. The two men, known for their extraordinary detail, had worked together on several Great Lakes side wheelers.

The men's smoking lounge on the *Detroit III*'s upper deck, known as the Gothic Room, was considered the highlight of Keil's masterpiece. It had a Tiffany stained-glass La Salle window and Gothic-style English oak details throughout. Some considered it the most beautiful room ever built on a ship.

Detroit III spent most of its days sailing between Detroit, Cleveland and Buffalo. According to the Detroit Historical Society, a typical Detroit-to-Buffalo trip left just before dinner and arrived the following morning.

Thousands of passengers enjoyed *Detroit III*'s splendor over its decades-long career, but in 1956, as the era of steamships was ending, the *Detroit III* was sold with plans to be scrapped.

First, it was stripped of its art, and everything that was salvageable was sold at auction, including the steering wheel and whistle.

According to Historic Detroit, a house painter from Cleveland named Frank Schmidt bought the interior of the Gothic Room, stained-glass window and all, and had it installed in the loft of a barn in a Cleveland suburb.

After Frank's death, his sister sold his maritime treasures to a restaurant-decorating firm in Cleveland that sold a large section of his collection to the Dossin Great Lakes Museum on Belle Isle, Michigan.

"By December 1966, a fundraising effort had raised $40,000 (about $290,000 today) to buy the ornate Gothic Room, whistles, murals and more and bring them back to Detroit," reads Historic Detroit.

> *The collection included more than seven tons of woodwork alone. The Great Lakes Maritime Institute spearheaded the effort to have part of the famed room installed in the Dossin. Kolowich, the last operator of the D&C vessels, gave the drive a big boost by donating thousands of invalidated D&C Navigation Company stock certificates, which were sent to those who donated $2 or more. The Daughters of the American Revolution donated $2,700 for the La Salle window, but most of the donations came from individual Detroiters eager to bring pieces of the beloved boats home.*

Volunteers spent thousands of hours restoring and installing the room, though not in its entirety nor in its exact original layout. According to the

Detroit Historical Society, "Stepping through its doors is like stepping back in time inside the reconstructed gentlemen's lounge of the *City of Detroit III*, with a window on the right side of the gallery set up as if you're looking out at the Detroit shore line in the early 1900s."

J.F. Reagan Grocery and Ship Supplier

In the early 1900s, the Port of Lorain, in the middle of Lake Erie's Ohio coastline, was a bustling watery highway of ship activity. Iron ore, coal, limestone, sand, gravel and stone were regularly loaded and unloaded in the harbor. Workers at the nearby American Ship Building Company's shipyard were busy building iron ore carriers to keep up with the growing demand of the steel industry.

Many ships traveling to Lorain came from the Upper Great Lakes and were running low on food and supplies by the time they reached Ohio waters. They knew they could count on the Reagan family, the main marine grocers in Lorain, to restock them when they got to the port.

The business started with James Francis Reagan, who, with Joseph Gawn, opened Reagan & Gawn Grocery on Broadway in 1905. According to a book compiled by the family, *Celebrating 100 Years of the Reagan Home: 1923–2023*, it was the same year Francis married Loretta Dineen, and they later had four children, Merla, Peg, Brendon and James Jr.

J.F. Reagan grocery store, 1930s. *Courtesy of Terry Reagan.*

In 1907, James Sr. dissolved his partnership with Gawn and opened J.F. Reagan Grocery on the Black River on the west side of the Erie Avenue Bridge, providing groceries and supplies to the boats of the Great Lakes Shipping Fleet. He opened a second store at the east end of the bridge, but both stores were destroyed by a deadly F4 tornado that swept through Lorain in 1924.

The store was rebuilt, and James Sr.'s children began working there when they were old enough. Eventually, his sons Brendon and James Jr. ran it (along with their children years later).

Dan Brady, of Brady Bunch of Lorain County Nostalgia, shared a 1940 article from the Lorain *Morning Journal* that describes how Brendon's job as assistant to his father, at thirty-two years old, often changed quickly from mundane to dangerous:

> *Young Reagan calls the harbor tug station, learns the S.S.* Queen City, *hauling ore from Duluth, Minn., to National Tube Co. in Lorain, is due at the breakwater in 20 minutes. Discarding white grocer's apron, Reagan hurries down to a dock back of the store on Black River, jumps into a two-cylindered cabin launch, maneuvers into stream, under the bridge and he's off for the Queen City.*

As he passed the Coast Guard station, he saw the triangular red storm warning for small craft at the top of the pole and warily eyed the sky. Suddenly, it began to thunder, and rain pelted him in the face as he steered toward the ship.

"Altho [*sic*] just late afternoon the guiding pier lights, which go on automatically only when dark enough, begin flashing—red stabs in the murk from the west pier, green from the east. Blasts from the freighter reveal its fleet, class and name—the S.S. *Queen City*, next to last in the Pittsburgh Steamship Co. fleet," the article continues.

Reagan pulled alongside the four-hundred-footer, tied up and climbed over the side. He headed down to the submarine galley, where he usually got an order from the freighter chef. But this time, the chef decided to wait to place his order until docking, so Brendon headed back empty-handed to his small boat and shoved off, thankfully with calmer waters. It was a standard day of work.

In addition to supplying food, the Reagans also helped sailors stay in touch with their wives, girlfriends and family.

Terry and Elaine Reagan on the shores of Lake Erie. *Photo by author.*

"Letters, cards and packages are mailed to lake-faring men on ships 'in care of Reagan's grocery, Lorain,'" reads the *Morning Journal* article. "J.F. Reagan laughs about the system, but explains that messages aren't the only things exchanged, 'Pictures, neckties, socks and other presents are handled in similar manner,' he says. 'When letters are not deliverable, we just forward them to the Detroit river [*sic*] station where all sailors can get their mail.'"

Terry Reagan (Brendon's son), who has four adult children and lives in Willoughby with his wife, Elaine, recalled working at the store as a teen. He said although people in the neighborhood shopped there for groceries, many of the items on the shelves were in large cans to fill the needs of the forty- to fifty-member crews on the ships.

In the 1950s, another grocery store opened nearby, and for about a decade, the Reagans had fierce competition. Whichever grocer could get to the ship first when it entered the harbor could get the order for their store.

The Reagan family knew the drill—they kept a close eye on the freighter schedule and stood watch from Grandma and Grandpa Reagan's backyard.

OYSTERS
BROCCOLI
Here's Where You Buy
HADDOCK
MACKEREL
SCALLOPS
OYSTERS
KRAFT CHEESE
World's Finest Cheeses
CRAX
NEW PEAS
OYSTERS
BIRDS EYE
FROSTED FOODS
Welch's
Grape Juice
Welch's

Inside Reagan grocery store. J.F. Reagan can be seen in the center, 1947. *Courtesy of Terry Reagan.*

They scanned the lake's horizon for ships, and once they saw one, they knew it would take one to two hours for the ship to get to the Lorain Harbor Lighthouse, depending on weather, and then it was time to get to work.

"My dad would go to his boat, the ship supply boat, and decide when he should leave the dock to get to the boat freighter when it hits the lighthouse," explained Terry. "When it got to the lighthouse the waves would be calm and he would pull alongside the freighter."

He would tie a line to the freighter while it was moving, go aboard and head to the galley. When the cook had an order, he would fill out a sheet with what was needed from the store.

"He would review the order and decide if they had what they needed," explained Terry. "They would get like a quarter of a cow, twenty-gallon cans of milk, no. 10 cans of canned goods."

After heading back to the river dock behind the store, his dad placed groceries and supplies in a wooden crate on his boat, the *J.F. Reagan*, and then carried it to the ship and hoisted it up.

"It was fun for me as a young kid to go with my dad on the boat, help him unload, go on the freighter once in a while," Terry recalled. "We also had residents who would call in orders for groceries. We would fill the order, and I would deliver the orders to the house in the Reagan van."

When the freighters arrived in Lorain, part of the crew was off duty, since they worked in shifts.

"For the ship to get to the place where they were going to unload the ore was two hours, so the crew that was off wanted to get off and go to the bars."

After dropping off the order, his dad went back and put the ladder up so crew could climb aboard his boat, and he took them to the dock so they could head to the bars for a few hours.

Sometimes, crew members lost track of time and missed the ship headed back to Duluth, so they called Terry's dad, Brendon, to tell him the ship had left the dock before they got there.

Brendon would pick them up to take them to the ship before it got to the lighthouse in the harbor, where they would climb aboard before it headed into open water.

Terry remembers sneaking off to some of those same bars with his friends in high school to buy quarts of beer. They drank the beer down by the river on his dad's dock and often threw the empty bottles into the river to hide the evidence. However, once, when Terry arrived to work at the store the next morning, the river had frozen overnight, and the bottles were sticking out of the ice.

Top: A Reagan ship supply boat at the docks after being built at Cleveland Stadium Boat Works, 1946. *Courtesy of Terry Reagan.*

Bottom: A J.F. Reagan ship supply boat loaded with supplies at a store dock on the Black River, early 1950s. *Courtesy of Terry Reagan.*

Terry quickly asked his brother to go down and knock the tops off the bottles before their dad could catch them, which he successfully did.

In the winter, when some of the ship chefs, who lived in Lorain, weren't working, Terry's grandpa hired them to cook a large meal for his family at his house on the lake.

"There was a guy who came in his full chef gear," recalled Terry. He said it not only entertained the Reagans but also helped the chef during the off months. It gave them a different kind of crew to serve.

Terry's wife, Elaine, grew up in Avon Lake, and although Terry was a well-known eligible bachelor in Lorain when they met, Elaine didn't know much about his family's legacy at first.

However, she was soon invited to the large formal parties held at Terry's parents' house.

"My family was well known and had high-end friends, so there was always a lot of commotion at my parents' house—with doctors—and my dad was just a guy for a food store, but my mother [Marcella] was in real estate. She would have these parties."

"I would get invited to these parties, and she had servers pass the food around with trays," recalled Elaine.

Elaine said after she and Terry were engaged, they planned to have a small wedding, but Terry's mom planned a huge country club wedding for them in Lorain in 1966. They received expensive gifts of china and wine glasses that they still have today.

At the same time, the bustling era of the Reagan grocery business was nearing an end.

According to Terry, U.S. Steel kept growing and owned most of the freighters from Duluth to Lorain. In the 1950s and '60s, the company decided to provide more food for freighter crew by setting up U.S. Steel ship supply stores along the way.

"So, that lowered the sales—took out the smaller guy because they were so dominant on the lake," explained Terry.

Freighters got larger and could move faster with less—going from, for example, five hundred feet long with thirty to forty crew members to one thousand feet long with only a ten-person crew. This made trips shorter, requiring fewer provisions.

By December 1979, Jim and Brendon Reagan, close to retirement age, were making their final deliveries on the Black River. The business had flourished for decades, ever since James Sr. started it. According to a 1979 article in *The Journal* (Lorain, OH), he first served the town folk "with a horse and wood-paneled wagon" and "later made deliveries by truck to housewives who could count on superior steaks and well-trimmed chops, and didn't mind paying a little bit more. And he also made deliveries to lake vessels, first by rowboat and outboard, and a sturdy, snub-nosed launch that was built to order in 1946."

Brothers Jim (*left*) and Brendon (*right*) working at the store. *Courtesy of the Reagan family.*

Automation and frozen foods also made local suppliers unnecessary for the ships, and an increase in street traffic, pedestrian hazards and limited parking decreased neighborhood sales.

After the store closed, its groceries and fixtures were auctioned off, but some items remain with the family, like the wooden sign that hung above the store door for decades. It represents generations of hardworking family members who all believed in putting their hopes and dreams into creating a successful legacy based on the name of the man who started it all: J.F. Reagan.

Years later, one of James Sr.'s grandsons, Chris Reagan, wrote a song called "Up the Black River" that captures those marine grocery days so well. Here's a portion of it:

Round three in the morning he answers the phone
It's a cook from a freighter with a gruff and quick tone
I haven't much time sir this crew's getting sour
We're dumping this coal; we'll be gone in four hours
It's late in the season we've just one last run
From here to Duluth before our work's done

Chorus:
So heave away boys, cast-off from the dock
Up the Black River before six o'clock
The skipper he's waitin', there's a schedule to keep
We've an order to fill brother before we can sleep

Into the night through the darkness and mist
They meet once again to assemble the list
No time do they waste, no machines do they use
Just their hands and their backs and the soles of their shoes

Chorus:
There's sugar and flour and canned goods and beef
And cases of beer to bring some relief
Like parts of a puzzle they fit together
And stow it on board for the trip up the river

Aeromarine Airways

Before the construction of modern freeways, when steamships were leisurely ferrying passengers and commercial flight was in its infancy, people could only dream of traveling from Detroit to Cleveland in less than two hours.

But on July 14, 1922, that changed when Aeromarine Airways, a little-known pioneering air carrier, began the first regularly scheduled passenger commercial flight in the United States between Cleveland and Detroit, making ninety-minute air travel between cities a reality.

"A shortcut across Lake Erie to avoid the circuitous journey via road or rail via Toledo, Ohio," said Paul Soprano on AviationCLE.com.

A 1922 Aeromarine brochure/timetable of the Great Lakes division reads:

> *Swift—Safe—Delightful—Boats fly only over the water; and generally, only a few feet above the water, hence a convenient landing space is always available.*
>
> *See the wondrous panorama as it unfolds beneath you like a magic carpet, with its villages nestling peacefully among the trees, like tiny toy towns. You can see more in a few minutes from the sky than you could in a year of ordinary travel.*

The "flying boats" were fixed-winged seaplanes with a hull that allowed them to land on water. They were designed and manufactured in Cleveland, and *Wolverine* and *Santa Maria* were the first two aircraft to inaugurate the Detroit–Cleveland service. Aeromarine operated from a floating dock/terminal in Cleveland Harbor, which, based on old pictures, was located between present-day city hall and the Cuyahoga County Courthouse.

On disembarking, passengers were greeted by an escort of twenty mounted police who transported them to a welcome party luncheon hosted by the Cleveland Chamber of Commerce, according to Transportation History.

A passenger named Peggy MacLean flew on the Aeromarine Airways hydroplane *Buckeye* between Detroit and Cleveland and described her experience to the *Detroit News*: "It's magic! If I could only make you feel my thrills and sensations you would agree that the world and the inventions of man have almost attained the sublime. It was like being in Heaven and looking benevolently down the little spot of earth known as the world."

The 1922 brochure coaxed potential travelers to try Aeromarine: "The enclosed cabin boat has seating capacity for eleven people in comfort. Forward cabin contains six wicker chairs and large observation cockpit. After cabin furnished as Club Compartment suitable for cards, special Writing Room or Lounge. The open cockpit boat has a seating capacity for four."

The Aeromarine Airways ticket office in the Hollenden Hotel, Cleveland, 1922. *Image from* Wings Over America, *by Harry Bruno.*

Aeromarine showed the first in-flight movie, titled *Howdy Chicago!*, to passengers on flights in 1921 and later experimented with radio entertainment aboard *Buckeye* after *Detroit News* staff added 150 pounds of radio receiving equipment to its rear cabin. "Despite the roar of the motors and speed of the aircraft, the morning concert show of WWJ radio was received clearly during the 90-minute flight," Soprano wrote. "The announcer sent greetings to the passengers and crew about the *Buckeye*, too."

The Ninety Minute Line ran two daily roundtrip flights from Detroit to Cleveland, covering ninety-five miles in ninety minutes, carrying only passengers and cargo. One-way fare cost $24 (about $400 today), compared to $9 fare by train and $5 by steamer.

Aeromarine Airways operated until only 1924, but according to Transportation History, it set pivotal standards for subsequent airlines for pilot training, maintenance programs and the seasonal rotation of equipment.

It's also credited with setting up the first U.S. airline ticket office at the Hollenden Hotel on East Ninth Street in Cleveland.

2

Heroes, Villains and Legendary Characters

Hero Inventor Garrett Morgan

Garrett Morgan was a legendary Cleveland entrepreneur and inventor who saved lives with his creations while overcoming obstacles.

Born in Kentucky in 1877 to parents who were formerly enslaved, Garrett received six years of education before he moved to Cincinnati at just fourteen years old. While he was there, he worked and hired a tutor to continue his education, according to the *Encyclopedia of Cleveland History*.

His granddaughter Sandra Morgan, of Cleveland, said, "Throughout his lifetime he was smart. He knew he was smart, and, in that regard, he knew that he stood apart from his siblings. Not that they weren't smart, but he had a unique talent. It was a recognized talent by family and friends and teachers that he had a unique ability, and it was nurtured. That was a blessing quite honestly and he was encouraged to be the best he could be."

In a time when many Black children would have been told to stop wasting their time with imagining, to work at a mill or factory instead, Garrett's thoughtfulness was encouraged, and he was given the freedom to tinker and create. Although Black students in Kentucky received only six years of education, Sandra believes they fit as much as they could into that time.

"So maybe he had access to rudimentary science—chemistry and biology, math and English," Sandra said. "Think of what it sparked in him that he was able to use the principles of chemistry and engineering in order to build and discover things that others have not."

Garrett was intrigued by the industrial excitement happening in Cleveland with entrepreneurs Thomas Edison and J.P. Morgan and decided to move there in 1895.

While working as a sewing machine adjuster for clothing manufacturers, he fell in love with his future wife, Czech immigrant Mary Hasek. The company didn't approve of their biracial relationship, so they left, and Garrett went into business for himself in 1907, "establishing a shop on W. 6th St. to repair and sell sewing machines," according to the *Encyclopedia of Cleveland History*.

In 1908, he and Mary were married, and they had three sons, John, Garrett Jr. (Sandra's father) and Cosmo.

His oldest son, John P., was named after J.P. Morgan, a dominating financier and the head of the banking firm that became J.P. Morgan and Co., after Garrett reached out to him in a creative way.

"My grandfather read that he [J.P. Morgan] was a sportsman and enjoyed hunting and so my grandfather got a couple of hunting dogs, nice ones, and had them delivered to J.P. Morgan with a note," explained Sandra. "He said, 'I understand you like to hunt. I am also an outdoorsman. I like horses and I like hunting. Please accept my gift of a couple of hunting dogs.'"

According to Sandra, after Garrett's first son was born, he sent a note to J.P. Morgan to tell him he had named his son after him and received a lovely note back with a savings bond for his son (which has never been cashed—the bond, signed by J.P. Morgan, remains in the family).

"It illustrates his guts and willingness to take a chance," said Sandra.

It was a theme that carried Garrett throughout his successful career.

"In 1909 he opened a tailoring shop; with 32 employees, he manufactured suits, dresses, and coats. In 1913 he organized the G.A. Morgan Hair Refining Co. to market a hair-straightening solution he had discovered by accident in 1905," reads the *Encyclopedia of Cleveland History*.

The discovery began at his shop. After noticing the fast-moving sewing needles were scorching the fabric, Garrett tried to figure out a solution. One day, while testing oil to use on the needles, his wife called him to lunch. According to Sandra, he wiped his oil-covered hands on a piece of lamb's wool, washed his hands and noticed the oil had smoothed the lamb's wool.

"He tried it on their dog—that was an Airedale—and noticed the hair was smooth too," explained Sandra. "So, then he went into the house and tried putting it on his own head, while my grandmother was saying, 'Stop! Don't put that on your head!' But he did it anyway."

Garrett realized he could market it as a hair straightener and went into the hair care business, developing the Garrett Morgan cream that was promoted as being gentle enough to use on beards and mustaches and was sold all over Ohio and the East Coast through the 1970s.

Sandra recalled an uncle telling her that they would all get together on Thursday nights to use the cream to get their hair slicked back to go to parties over the weekend.

Around that time, Garrett was inventing what would become one of his greatest creations: a safety helmet breathing device to protect the wearer from smoke and ammonia. It was introduced in 1912 and patented in 1914, just in time to help saves lives during a major disaster below Lake Erie.

According to the *Encyclopedia of Cleveland History*:

> *In 1896 a new 9' tunnel extending over 4 mi. into the lake was begun in order to bring fresh water into a newly built pumping station at Kirtland St. (E. 49th St.). Five of the 6 disasters occurred as a result of its construction. Two gas explosions in 1898, and one each in 1901 and 1902, took the lives of 28 tunnel workers. On 4 Aug. 1901, a fire was ignited by cinders from a boiler stack in a temporary crib built to house the workers; 5 men burned to death, 3 drowned trying to escape the crib, and 1 rescuer lost his life trying to reach workmen in the tunnel. The work was completed in 1904. The final disaster took place 12 years later, on 24 July 1916, when workmen digging in a 10' wide tunnel hit a pocket of natural gas. A spark triggered an explosion, killing 11 men and 10 would-be rescuers who were overcome by gas when they entered the pressurized tunnel.*

Garrett and his brother Frank heroically arrived at the scene with the breathing device/safety hoods and entered the gas-filled tunnel at the request of the Cleveland Police. They descended into the tunnel with the devices, rescued two workers and brought back four bodies.

However, for years, Garrett received very little recognition for his heroism, which his granddaughter believes was due to prejudice.

According to Brittany Moseley's 2023 article in the Ohio History Connection's *Echoes* magazine:

> *In an October 1917 letter to then–Cleveland Mayor Harry Davis, Morgan accuses the mayor of depriving him "of the rewards which my work has merited, in connection with the recent Lake Erie Tunnel disaster." He goes on to ask why the mayor chose to remain silent when the Carnegie Hero Fund Commission gave awards to other men who assisted with the tunnel rescue but not Morgan.*

Years later, Garrett received various awards, according to a 1958 *Cleveland Call and Post* article, including "a diamond-studded medal to 'Cleveland's most honored and bravest citizen, for going five miles out in Lake Erie and 250 feet under the bottom of the Lake."

"G.A. Morgan's Gas Mask and Smoke Protector" inspired the gas masks used by U.S. troops during World War I. The design was eventually bought by the American-LaFrance Fire Engine Co. in Elmira, New York.

Another invention that helped make the world safer was his three-way traffic light that used a third cautionary signal between "stop" and "go." As detailed in my book *Hidden History of Lake County, Ohio*, it was tested in Willoughby, Ohio, where a replica of his invention exists. He sold his traffic light patent to General Electric in 1923 for $40,000.

He was also a leader in the Black community, founding the weekly newspaper *Cleveland Call* and the Cleveland Association of Colored Men, and he decided to invest the money he made on his traffic light invention into a 121-acre farm south of Wakeman along the Vermilion River.

"His Wakeman Country Club operated between 1924 and sometime in the war years of the early 1940s," says Green Book Cleveland. "Members of the club, drawn largely from Cleveland, bought private lots with the intent to build cottages. The club offered dining in its Chicken Shack, dancing, horseback riding, hunting, fishing and even boxing exhibitions."

It allowed Garrett, who was struggling with health problems, including vision loss due to glaucoma, to slow down and enjoy himself.

Sandra said her grandfather died when she was only two years old, but she has heard a lot about him—he was thoughtful, intense and serious, not much of a jokester.

"My dad talked about him. And he and my Uncle Cosmo were roughhousing and being a nuisance, and my grandfather was like, 'Cut it out, stop that.' And they were packing up to go to the farm and he threw a pound of butter down the stairs, and it hit the wall and completely flattened and they stopped what they were doing," recalled Sandra. "But at the same time, he was indulgent and allowed them to do things that they wanted."

Sandra said when it came to animals, Garrett was a softie; his children grew up with pets at the Wakeman farm. "When the police would retire

Firemen With Safety Hoods Make Test at Headquarters

Hoods that cover the head, enabling firemen to enter rooms filled with smoke and fumes, were given a test by B. J. McConnell, chief of the fire department, and pronounced a success.

The hoods are so arranged the firemen can breathe pure air near the floor or ground no matter how dense the smoke may be. The hoods are made of canvas and rubber and can be quickly slipped over the head. Two long tubes that converge into one, the end of which drags on the ground, admit fresh air.

The test was made by George Mason, demonstrator and fire official. Mason wore the cap for thirty-seven minutes in a room at headquarters which had been filled with smoke and gas from burning formaldehyde, sulphur and rags.

Chief McConnell said he may make a recommendation for the purchase of several of the hoods for use in the department.

Opposite: Garrett Morgan with his award. *Courtesy of the Cleveland Public Library/photograph collection.*

Above: Firemen testing out Morgan's safety hoods, November 16, 1913. *From the* Buffalo Courier.

horses, he would take them to save them and brought them to the farm. They always had horses. He had dogs—loved dogs—as pets. He loved the horses and took care of them, and they grew up to be loving animals."

Garrett also planted his wife an apple orchard, and she used those apples to make apple pie and applesauce for the family for years.

In his later years, Garrett was still inventing, telling the *Call and Post* in 1958 that new ideas "constantly creep into my mind." One of his most unusual inventions, according to the article, was a device to raise a corpse in a casket:

> *Here's how the device would work. A small tubular affair would be placed in the coffin underneath the cadaver. Pressure on a button would automatically force the body into an upright position, enabling those viewing the remains to shake the hand as they would file past....*
>
> *"But consultation with local undertakers forced me to abandon the idea," Morgan said. "They told me it would be a surefire way of emptying the funeral service area in a hurry—to see the body rising by itself," he chuckled.*

In 1956, Garrett was granted another patent for a new hair curler for women. Although he was 90 percent blind by then, he was determined to create.

Garrett had the right combination of thoughtfulness, creativity and passion to invent things that changed our world, and his granddaughter Sandra feels he should be recognized globally. "His contributions to public safety are irrefutable and they are legacy projects and long-lasting. And even more significant because of the times he was contributing and the tools he had to work with. I think if he could do it with a sixth-grade education, that opens the door for all of us. It should give all of us more than hope; it should allow us all to think big and broadly and to follow our dreams no matter what they are."

America's First Female Deep-Sea Diver

In 1917, when diving for shipwrecks in Lake Erie was uncommon for men and unheard of for women, Margaret Campbell Goodman was determined to find treasure. She was believed to be the only female deep-sea diver of her time and the only woman in the world in the salvage business.

Margaret Campbell Goodman, 1923. *Library of Congress.*

Margaret had her eyes set on the wreck of the steamship *Pewabic*, which sank in Lake Huron's Thunder Bay, near Michigan, after it collided with its sister ship, *Meteor*, in 1865, resulting in the deaths of 155 passengers.

According to a 1934 *Brooklyn Eagle* article, Margaret organized a salvage company in Toledo, chartered boats and acquired the rights to a newly invented manganese bronze diving suit before heading to the wreck.

"I was always a dreamer," she said in a 1921 *Washington Herald* article. "And I can hardly remember when I first began to dream that there was a fortune in deep sea salvage. The reality came when I first became interested in a suit of diving armor being demonstrated about four years ago at Grand Traverse Bay, Michigan."

The 1921 article explained that the suits Margaret used in her 1917 expedition were an improved design that provided air from a tank "in a continuous current after being breathed through a cartridge containing caustic soda for elimination of carbonic gas" instead of pumping air directly down to the diver. "During tests of the suit, divers working for her went down 361 feet to a depth where the pressure was 156 pounds to the square inch, thereby setting a new world's record in this field," the 1934 article reads.

Goodman led the group to the 180-foot-deep wreck, and in that first season, divers recovered one hundred tons of copper and one hundred tons of pig-iron, along with many relics from the *Pewabic*'s hull, according to the *Brooklyn Eagle*.

"As soon as the news of how we were succeeding flashed abroad, I had letters from people all over the country who had lost relatives in the disaster, begging me to send some souvenir of their loved ones," Margaret explained.

One article reads, "She startled many who read of her exploits in donning a suit and exporting the sea bottom, thereby becoming America's first woman deep-sea diver."

Many people thought this was quite outlandish, which Goodman resented.

"I have also been annoyed being written off as merely a woman diver, out for the sensational part of it. I am engaged in the salvage business and I am in it for the money, but I am not a freak and do not relish being treated as one," she stated in a 1921 article.

In 1934, nearly two decades after Margaret's *Pewabic* expedition, when she was middle-aged, she planned to begin a new salvage expedition to Lake Erie. "I feel better than I have for several years," she said. "My health is good and I am ready to start once more." She told the newspaper that there is no difference of physique that would prevent a woman from diving as well as a man. "So long as they are not full-blooded or the victims of high blood pressure, they can do this dangerous job."

Although Margaret enjoyed diving in the Great Lakes, she lived at 203 Allen Avenue, Gerritsen Beach, in Brooklyn, New York, by a much larger body of water, the Atlantic Ocean.

Margaret was only four feet, nine inches tall and weighed about one hundred pounds. Once, when she wanted to practice diving in the ocean to keep herself in "diving trim," she couldn't find a suit that was small enough.

Although contracts with the owners of the wrecked vessel were signed, Margaret wasn't taking the chance of revealing the name of the ship she planned to dive to or its whereabouts. According to the 1934 article, that's because she once arrived at a Great Lakes wreck she intended to dive only to find another salvager already there. "She promptly started court proceedings against him, she recalls. The other treasure hunter did not know the difference between salvaging in the ocean, where the law is finders' keepers, and in the Great Lakes where a wreck belongs to its owner," the article reads.

She Has Her Ups and Downs

MRS. MARGARET CAMPBELL GOODMAN, who claims she is the world's only woman diver, is pleased because of the speed with which she located the wreck on the bottom of Lake Erie from which she hopes to recover a small fortune in logs. Mrs Goodman goes in for extremes; on Saturday she flew the spotting plane herself and tomorrow expects to don a diving suit and direct operations off a point some 10 miles east of Wheatley.

Margaret Campbell Goodman in her pilot gear, October 15, 1934. *From the* Windsor Star, *a division of Postmedia Network Inc.*

A few months later, Margaret was once again making headlines in the *Windsor Star*, wearing pilot goggles and a trench coat. It turns out the adventurer was also a pilot, and from the sky, she located the wreck of the *New Brunswick*, which had sunk in 1859 near Leamington, Ontario.

According to Shipwreck World, the *New Brunswick* was hauling eighteen thousand bushels of wheat from Chicago to Liverpool, England, in 1847 in the first direct shipment of grain made by a Great Lakes vessel to Europe. More than a decade later, it sank in Lake Erie during a fierce August gale, carrying a full cargo of valuable black walnut and white oak lumber (valued at $250,000 to $500,000 in 1934) offshore of Point Pelee. Only four of the nine crew members survived by clinging to a raft they constructed from the ship's debris.

In October 1934, Margaret planned to direct her crew to bring up the valuable cargo.

"Mrs. Goodman herself was at the controls of the airplane in the flight Saturday which resulted in the location of the sunken schooner a few moments after she had taken off. Careful cross-bearings of the location were taken in case the buoy dropped at the spot should drift," reads the article.

After the flight, Mr. and Mrs. Joseph Dawson, who lived on the lake shore where the ship foundered seventy-five years earlier, shared details with Margaret that had been passed down by Joseph's father, who lived there before them. Joseph's father told him that, contradictory to what had been reported for years, the crew survived, except for one Black man whose body washed ashore after the wreck.

"The masts of the schooner stood above water from August until the lake ice carried them out the next spring, and during the winter many farmers from the vicinity walked over the ice to the boat and secured portions of sail cloth from which mittens were made. Mr. and Mrs. Dawson still have a bit of the sail in their possession," according to the *Windsor Star*.

A 1935 *Windsor Star* article reported that after locating the wreck via plane, Margaret "became enmeshed in a tangle of difficulties with her backers and the heirs of the owners."

By 1938, a *Star Phoenix* article explained that Margaret, then sixty-five, was once again planning to salvage the lumber. "She's angry at the diver, Jack Browne of Milwaukee, who has announced he will also seek the treasure," reads the article. "'Experts tell me the wood actually improves under water,' Mrs. Goodman said. 'I should be inside the hull before another month passes. That young fellow Browne will not touch that ship so long as I have my contract.'"

Margaret again had a contract with the estate of the ship's owner, Baron Herbert, since his eighty-four-year-old son had little interest in the venture.

It's unclear if Margaret did go back to try to find the ship or if the heirs of the ship's owner decided they wanted to be the ones to hold the contract to dive for the lumber, but the wood wasn't raised from the wreck until 1980, when Mike Dilts, who then owned the salvage rights, directed the search operation.

According to Shipwreck World, Dilts's team found the ship using side scan sonar and recovered artifacts and fifty-five-foot-long, twenty-two-inch-square logs.

Margaret may not have retrieved the lumber like she hoped, but her bravery and tenacity made her legendary and paved the way for future women divers. She was proud of her role as a scuba diver, and according to the *Unionville Crescent* in 1935, she said the only other women who showed interest in donning a wet suit and diving were publicity-seeking movie actresses. "Scoffing at the thought that diving is too tough a profession for women, she exclaimed: 'Why, women could compete successfully with Navy divers! They are brave enough if given the opportunity. But I suppose they never will get into the navy ranks as divers. It's not the atmosphere for a woman.'"

Margaret was also a well-known writer in her time. She wrote for newspapers, spoke at conventions and contributed a section to the book *Careers for Women*, published by Houghton-Mifflin. She even helped found a women's magazine, *The Owelet*.

When Margaret wasn't busy organizing treasure expeditions or diving, she enjoyed writing poems and plays in her little cottage by the sea, likely also staring out at the water, dreaming of her next adventure.

Middle Island Club

The Lake Erie islands hold many secrets of their past. Some are inhabited tourist destinations, while others remain mostly desolate. Middle Island is a small, wooded island that sits just over the boundary line on the Canadian side of Lake Erie. Today, very few visit the island except for the occasional curious boater, perhaps looking for the treasure it was said to once hold. But in the 1930s, it was filled with activity—some, of the illegal variety.

"Sitting atop a rocky shoreline outcropping, the rotted-out hull of a long-forgotten fishing boat overlooks the aquamarine shallows," wrote Craig Mitchell in a 2023 Outdoor Canada article. "Nearby, an old car, brought over back when the lake would freeze solid, is slowly being reclaimed by Mother Nature. And just inside the treeline, you'll find the ruins of the once great Lake Erie Fishing Club, founded by Italian-American gangster Joe Roscoe."

According to FBI Director J. Edgar Hoover, Roscoe was "the reputed gambling king of Toledo."

"Like the stereotypical Hollywood gangster, Roscoe was also fond of aliases, and went under several, among them Vedo, Joseph Rosso, and Joseph Cole," wrote Chad Fraser in *Lake Erie Stories: Struggle and Survival on a Freshwater Ocean.* "Dark rumours always seemed to surround Roscoe, whom the January 28, 1937, *Toledo Blade* boldly referred to as a 'mysterious underworld character.' Most of them circulated around the gambling houses in Toledo."

Roscoe was said to be involved in rumrunning during Prohibition and sought out Middle Island as a safe spot for his endeavor.

In the early 1900s, according to Mitchell, it was regarded as the "fresh water fishing capital of the world," due to its plentiful walleye, whitefish, lake sturgeon and blue pike (now extinct). But after Roscoe took over the island, it was said to have a new reputation as a cover for illicit activities and as a rumrunning waypoint.

Behind the fishing façade, Roscoe built a compound of docks, maintenance sheds, staff houses and an airstrip, but the hotel casino was what drew the masses.

"It comprised a lavish seven-room mansion, complete with electricity, running water and grandiose architecture adorned with extravagant art and décor," wrote Mitchell. "The focal point and main attraction was the basement, carved out of solid limestone, with a casino fit for the Vegas strip. Roulette, slot machines, cards and craps were apparently the favourite games

The Middle Island Club. *Courtesy of* The History of Middle Island, Ontario, *by Michael Gora.*

of the day. Former groundskeeper Thomas McCormick recalls the building still had the craps table sitting in the basement when he worked on the island in the 1970s. 'It was a beautiful place,' he says."

The island attracted the kings of the underworld, including gangster Al Capone, who was said to be an avid fisherman. In fact, secret compartments were rumored to be built into the building, holding Capone's illegally obtained hidden fortunes. (People have gone back to search the ruins over the years, but to no avail.)

For years, Roscoe was said to stay off authorities' radar by offering access to his Lake Erie Fishing Club as an exclusive bribe. According to Fraser, journalists, police officers, judges and public officials frequented the island, where they were plied with offers of fishing, gambling and all the alcohol they could drink.

"If bribes weren't enough to sway someone's opinion or guarantee their silence, a fishing trip into the wild waters of Lake Erie provided an excellent opportunity to eliminate any opposition," wrote Fraser.

One of Roscoe's underworld friends, and a frequent guest on Middle Island, was Alvin "Creepy" Karpis. On one such fateful fishing trip, Karpis reportedly killed off the very doctor he'd hired to remove his fingerprints. While out celebrating with Karpis following the successful procedure, Dr. Joseph Moran was overheard saying, "I've got you guys in the palm of my hand." Not long after, Karpis invited the doctor to go fishing, and that was the last time he was seen alive. Moran was later found washed up on a beach in Ontario.

The big money maker for these criminals was allegedly transporting booze. Their fishing knowledge gave them an edge, because they understood the waterways and knew the hidden obstacles they needed to avoid.

In *Ohio Lighthouses*, Wil and Pat O'Connell wrote it was rumored that rum runners operating a fishing boat ferrying whiskey from Middle Island to Put-In-Bay could make up to $10,000 a month.

Authorities began to upgrade Coast Guard and police speedboats to outrun them. So, smugglers increased the speeds of their own boats. Roscoe had a speedboat called *Rainbow* that "sported a 12-cylinder, 500-horsepower engine, propelling it much faster than any police boat of the day," according to Mitchell.

Middle Island caretaker's cottage. *Courtesy of* The History of Middle Island, Ontario, *by Michael Gora.*

Local historian and author Michael Gora wrote the book *The History of Middle Island, Ontario*, published in 2024. In it, he states that some Americans visited Middle Island via a popular boat shuttle from Port Clinton during Prohibition because it had a liquor license. However, he disagrees with the claims it had ties to illegal rumrunning because he hasn't found evidence the owners of the island were involved in any illegal island activities other than gambling. "It was natural for visitors to the island to try to bring a bit of illegal liquor back into the U.S.," he wrote. "In 1929, Canadian authorities did shut down the liquor sales there briefly, but that was because of a technical violation of the valid liquor license the island had, and the liquor sales were restarted very soon again, legally. From the perspective of the Canadian authorities, the activities there during Prohibition were generally legal."

Michael wrote the FBI was certainly interested in who was going to Middle Island and wanted to know if gangsters were hanging out there. In 1937, the FBI finally caught Roscoe when he helped gangsters "Creepy" Karpis and Harry Campbell after they held up a mail train in Garretsville, Ohio, and took off with $34,000 in cash and $11,650 in bonds, according to a 1937 *Rochester Journal* article. Roscoe, accused of hiding the pair in his Adams Street apartment in Toledo, pleaded guilty and was sentenced to seven and a half years in a prison.

After being released, he returned to Toledo. In the 1960s, shortly before his death, he sold Middle Island and his fishing club, which had transitioned to become a locale for outdoor enthusiasts and businesspeople.

The island is now a wildlife sanctuary, home cormorants and snakes, as part of Point Pelee National Park. Curious tourists still visit the ruins of the long-gone Lake Erie Fishing Club, including treasure-seekers hoping to find Capone's rumored hidden treasure.

Joe Root: Hermit of Presque Isle

Joe Root, of Erie, Pennsylvania, is a legendary character who was said to live in a wooden crate on the shores of Presque Isle peninsula, wearing worn clothes and living off the land on a diet of raw fish and berries.

Ann Silverthorn shared a description of Joe from John G. Carney's book, *Tales of Old Erie,* on her blog:

Joe Root on Presque Isle, 1910. *Courtesy of Hagen History Center.*

> *He had the appearance of a dreamer. He would sit and stare out on the water for hours at a time. With all that sitting and staring, Joe didn't have much use for personal hygiene. His hair was long and stringy, he didn't shave or wash, and he was crawling with lice. He wore second-hand clothing, and his favorite item was an old bear-skin coat.*

In a 2023 Hagen History Center blog, Andrew Applebee shared details of the hermit of Presque Isle:

> *Joe Root was born in 1858 at the Erie County Poorhouse near what is now west 26th Street and Pittsburgh Avenue. His mother Susan toiled as a fisherwoman on the banks of the old canal at West 12th and Poplar Streets. Circus organizers and showmen used the canal to move their shows around the area. It is speculated that here Joe learned the art of ventriloquism which became a signature trick of his. Joe soon took up fishing and as a boy worked for Gilson Johnson near Fairview. Still in his teens and for unknown reasons Joe dropped out of society and took up residency on Presque Isle. At the time the Peninsula was desolate and wild which may have enticed the young Root. Not much else is known about his youth and there are no records of him until his mid-thirties.*

Although he lived alone, he was known to be social. He enjoyed teaching children how to fish and catch turtles and could be seen on the fringes of summer picnics.

Applebee included Herbert Spencer's memory of a late afternoon picnic run-in with Joe Root:

> *The shadows of the big oaks lengthened towards the east, and we trudged into the grove, walking on a hushed path of pine needles and last year's oak leaves. Just as the heavy picnic baskets were placed strategically about, ready for a sudden assault, the bushes parted and without a sound Joe Root stepped into our group. His clothes and mediaeval hat, quietly soft spoken, with a smile that all children loved, and their elders envied. His exit was equally dramatic, he simply vanished without a sound, usually after accepting all the food he could carry. Between entrance and exit, Joe the born clown, entertained his audience.*

He earned money by bartering goods he collected off the street and performing his ventriloquism act, in which he predicted the weather forecast through the medium of a hollow log. He then headed to a bar for a warm meal and to entertain businessmen with his ideas for businesses to be built along the peninsula, such as feather factories, balloon farms and even a circus. However, he never convinced anyone to fund them.

In 1903, when Joe was accused of stealing fishing tackle from a boathouse, so many people came to the trial to testify to Joe's honesty that the charges were dropped. Yet not everyone liked Joe, and some believed he might have tried to claim squatter's rights (legal ownership of a property that was never paid for after living on it for an extended time) on Presque Isle, but he denied ever wanting to own the peninsula. Then in 1910, a group of social workers removed him from his home. According to Silverthorn, they thought that since Joe was older and unable to care for himself, they should convince him to "visit" the county home, but once he was there, he missed the freedom of the peninsula and was described as acting like a caged animal. As his behavior became more unmanageable, he was transferred to Warren State Hospital, where he died in 1912.

For about two decades, beginning in 1999, Joe Root's Grill, near the entrance to the peninsula, stood as an homage to Presque Isle's most beloved hermit.

3

Lighthouses and Landmarks

Marblehead Lighthouse's Hidden Height

Marblehead Lighthouse has been a beacon on Lake Erie since 1822. It has stood on the western edge of Sandusky Bay, guiding ships through a shallow and treacherous stretch of water, since before the Village of Marblehead was founded in 1891.

It's the oldest continuously running lighthouse on the Great Lakes and one of the most recognizable.

Several years ago, it celebrated its two hundredth anniversary, and the Marblehead Lighthouse Historical Society volunteers conducted in-depth research and shared its colorful history with visitors, including that of the fifteen Marblehead Lighthouse keepers, including two women, from 1822 to 1943, when the U.S. Coast Guard took over. This history includes stories of nearby shipwrecks and lighthouse structural changes.

But one piece of information was always missing, according to Lorrie Halblaub, a volunteer archivist with the Marblehead Lighthouse Historical Society: "Before now, we never knew how tall the lighthouse is," she explained. "The Coast Guard measures lights from the water to the light source because that's what mariners need to know but as for the whole light from top to bottom, we had no clue. I have seen figures from forty feet to eighty feet and in between."

She said getting to the bottom of this mystery was an interesting process. She found that the original stone tower, built in 1821 with five-foot-thick

Right: Marblehead Lighthouse, 1881–96. *Author's collection.*

Below: Marblehead Lighthouse, 1903–29. *Author's collection.*

walls, was fifty-five feet tall, but today, the lighthouse is much taller. According to Lorrie, in 1897, the top of the lighthouse was remodeled to accommodate the size of a new 3.5-order Fresnel ordered from Bernard and Turenne Co. in Paris, France. The original lighthouse was too narrow at the top to house the new lens, so the stone was removed to expand the space.

"The iron lantern on the tower which weighs about ten tons is now suspended in the air about seventy-five feet above the ground while the top of the tower is being removed to give room for a new brick top which forms a watch room with shelves, closets and circular stairs to the lantern," reads an 1897 *Sandusky Daily Register* article Lorrie tracked down.

Over eight feet of the fifty-five-foot-tall tower was removed and replaced with a circular brick liner that went from the ground up to fifty-four feet, five inches. "This liner formed the inside walls that the iron staircase is attached to today. The stone section and the brick section are connected by the band of something, maybe concrete. After this change, workers replaced the old deck and railing and old lantern," Lorrie explained.

Over the next few years, a new spiral iron staircase replaced the old pine steps, and six feet, eleven and a half inches of circular brick were added to the tower, making it sixty-one feet, four and a half inches tall. The old lantern was once again reinstalled, and a new deck was added.

Renovations continued in 1901, when a new lantern (reused from the decommissioned Erie Land Light in Pennsylvania) was placed on top of the brick with a second smaller deck and railing built around it. Lorrie believes the light came with the ten-sided dome on top of the lantern, which changed the top shape from an octagon to a decagon, while adding three and a half feet.

The dome of the lighthouse was painted for its two hundredth anniversary, but the shade wasn't quite right, leaning more toward pink than the signature red. So, in the spring of 2024, when the dome of the lighthouse was repainted a vibrant red, the ventilator and lightning rod were measured using a drone, and the lighthouse's current height was determined to be seventy-seven feet, eight and one-eighth inches.

According to the Marblehead Lighthouse Historical Society, the lighthouse is built of native limestone, originally left bare and then covered with gunite (a fine concrete that can be sprayed on) and later stucco. However, this means the surface must be regularly maintained. The historical society said experts believe the lighthouse has lasted so long and withstood severe weather conditions because it was built on a bedrock of stone that was so fine it was nearly waterproof. And the builder, William

Marblehead Lighthouse at night, 1930. *Author's collection.*

Kelly, used the correct mortar consistency, which was allowed to cure before heavy light equipment was installed.

Today, the lighthouse is part of a state park that is one of the most popular in Ohio. The grounds also have an 1880s-era keeper's house that houses a museum and gift shop and a replica of Marblehead's 1876 Lifesaving Station that was a precursor to the Coast Guard. (The original station was located about a mile away on the site of the current Coast Guard station, which is one of the busiest on the Great Lakes, according to Susan Glaser's Cleveland.com article "Marblehead Lighthouse Celebrates 200 Years.")

But for many, the best thing about the park is climbing those seventy-seven steps to the top, when the lighthouse is open to the public in warm weather months, to see the panoramic view that includes Cedar Point to the east and Kelleys Island and Put-in-Bay to the north. It allows you to imagine how treacherous the construction work must have been in those early days and what those lighthouse keepers must have experienced so many years ago.

HAUNTED DUNKIRK LIGHTHOUSE

The first shots in the War of 1812 were said to have been fired at Point Gratiot, in Dunkirk, New York, where the Dunkirk Lighthouse was built fifteen years later.

"This light acted in tandem with a pier head beacon to guide ships to the safety of the Dunkirk Harbor," according to the Dunkirk Lighthouse website. "The tower was refitted with a 3rd-order Fresnel lens and lantern in 1857."

Nearly half a century after it was built, the tower was reported to be in precarious condition and was threatened by erosion, so about a year later, a sixty-one-foot tower and Victorian residence were built to replace the tower and still stand today.

The lighthouse's website lists more than a dozen keepers who served between 1827 and 1961. During that time, the light's ties to historical events continued. Several shipwrecks occurred nearby, including those of the lake's first steamboat, *Walk-in-the-Water*, which was lost to a storm in 1821, and the steamer *Erie*, which caught on fire and sank two decades later. According to the Dunkirk Lighthouse website, in 1897, the freighter *Idaho* sank nearby, and some of its cargo, including slabs of chocolate for Christmas, were recovered by locals.

Point Gratiot Lighthouse, Dunkirk, New York, 1917. *Author's collection.*

There's also a legend that the first soldier killed at the Battle of Gettysburg in the Civil War, Corporal Cyrus Jones, was buried on the grounds of the lighthouse. Although Corporal Jones called Dunkirk home before serving, he was buried in the Gettysburg National Cemetery.

Perhaps it's these layers of history that lead some to believe this long-standing lighthouse is haunted by the ghosts of former keepers, those who lost their lives in nearby wrecks or even spirits associated with the many historic and military items housed in its museum.

In a 2021 interview with Buffalo's WIVB reporter Gabrielle Mediak, Dave Briska, who has led tours on the grounds for years, shared some stories: "You'll hear music playing, people talking, doors open and close."

One lighthouse paranormal investigation resulted in the image of an orb that appears to show part of a face. Dave recognized the features in the orb right away as those of Peter Dempsey, who was lighthouse keeper from 1885 to 1902, and his image is displayed in the lighthouse.

Dave believes some of the ghosts include the spirits of a man named Charlie and several children. "The lighthouse keeper and Charlie went out to rescue these children in Lake Erie," he told Mediak. "Charlie and the two children drowned, and since that time, they've spent all their time here at the house."

According to a 2020 interview with Mike Randall at Buffalo's WKBW, Dave believes Charlie's ghost once nudged him when he was standing at a window on the property. And another time, when Dave was opening the building for the season, he could clearly hear a voice say, "Get out!"

Dave also believes the children like to tag along with visitors, and he said they have been heard rolling a ball across the dining room floor.

Some of the most common paranormal happenings at the lighthouse include visitors hearing disembodied voices and footsteps that follow them up the staircases, according to the website Only in Your State. Some people hear a strange humming noise, while others have even been touched and grabbed by an unseen figure when they are alone in the tower and keeper's house.

Turtle Island Lighthouse

Turtle Island, which borders Michigan and Ohio in Lake Erie, was named after the Native war chief Little Turtle.

According to the Lighthouse Friends website, the nearly seven-acre island served as a fort during the Battle of 1794, but the U.S. government no longer needed it by 1827, so it was auctioned off.

As industry grew in Toledo, the government decided a navigational aid was needed in Maumee Bay, since the main shipping channel ran south of Turtle Island. So, in 1831, the government bought the island back with money appropriated from Congress to build a lighthouse and combat erosion.

The forty-two-foot-tall lighthouse, along with a keeper's dwelling, was built on Turtle Island in 1832, but a few years later, Lake Erie's water level rose, reducing the island from about seven acres to just over one acre.

In a desperate attempt to preserve the island, the government reduced the island to about a half an acre by "driving a double row of piles around a portion of the island and then using the area outside the piles as fill to elevate the land inside the piles. Good soil was then brought in from the mainland to cover the island," according to LighthouseFriends.com.

This protected the lighthouse for the next two decades, but the lamps and reflectors were in terrible condition by 1857, so a 4th-order Fresnel lens was installed in the lantern room.

After the Civil War, Congress appropriated money to build a new forty-five-foot-tall square lighthouse with a cast-iron staircase on Turtle Island.

It was attached to a one-and-a-half-story keeper's dwelling, was capped with a black lantern and retained the former Fresnel lens. It shone for the first time in 1866.

As shipping on Lake Erie grew, the shipping lane off Turtle Island was too shallow to accommodate the larger ships sailing to and from Toledo. "A new straight channel with a width of 400 feet and a depth of 21 feet was dredged through Maumee Bay, and Toledo Harbor Lighthouse was constructed atop a pier in Lake Erie to mark the entrance to the channel," reads LighthouseFriends.com.

An April 27, 1904 article in the *Plain Dealer* reported the lighthouse board decided to discontinue the Turtle Island light because it was misleading to commercial vessels that used only the main channel: "With the completion of Toledo Harbor Lighthouse, Turtle Island was decommissioned on May 15, 1904. Toledo Harbor Lighthouse was not activated until eight days later, and mariners were irate that the entrance was left unmarked during that period. A newspaper article said that mariners believed 'horse sense' should have caused officials to place the new light in service before deactivating the old one."

The lighthouse was sold, and the lens was removed and shipped to the lighthouse depot in Buffalo; however, its fate is unknown.

A few decades later, in March 1924, Turtle Island was the site of an airplane crash, according to the *Plain Dealer*: "Shifting wind this afternoon filled the channel at the mouth of Maumee Bay with drifting ice and made it impossible to recover an army pursuit plane that plunged into Lake Erie, near Turtle Island lighthouse last Friday." Engine trouble forced the pilot to try to land on the ice-covered lake, but it crashed through the ice. He and a recruit passenger survived and walked two miles to shore on Turtle Island.

The lighthouse was also a gathering place, according to the Lighthouse Friends website. A 1929 story in the *Toledo Blade* reported, "Captain John Skeldon of Toledo recalls piloting, immediately after his return from the Civil War, a party of young people to the island for a dancing party on the tug GEORGE R. HAND shortly after the completion of the lighthouse. They were guests of the lightkeeper."

In the 1930s, the island was nearly revitalized as a summer yacht club, but it was decided the island was too remote for members.

A fierce storm in 1965 blew the lighthouse's lantern off, and vandalism increased in the early 1970s, when the windows and steel staircase were stolen, according to a 1997 *Times-Gazette* article by Mitch Weiss.

Inside the ruins of the Turtle Island Lighthouse. *Courtesy of Sam Rotroff.*

Ruins of the Turtle Island Lighthouse. *Courtesy of Sam Rotroff.*

The island is currently privately owned, but some locals still venture over, including Sam Rotroff of Toledo, known as "Camping with Sam Bananas" on his YouTube channel, who paddled the mile or so across Lake Erie to camp overnight on Turtle Island in 2024. While there, he found remnants of the lighthouse, including bricks and an old rusty crane.

"The coolest-looking thing is the lighthouse, but it's just a shell. There are the ruins of the old buildings which are neat. I'd say the most interesting things are the crane that sits right on the water's edge," Sam explained. "Also, the giant circular cement barrier that was built to slow erosion is pretty cool. There is graffiti on it that dates back over 100 years."

Treasure Hunt at Turtle Island

It was the Fourth of July weekend in 1954, and brothers Jim (eleven), Michael (nine) and Terry (eight) Murray of Toledo were visiting their uncle Bill and aunt Katie Gray in Point Place (in northeast Toledo).

The Grays lived on Edgewater Drive near 124th Street, overlooking Maumee Bay, and the Murray brothers enjoyed playing near the water. They shared their memories of one thrilling outing with me: "Terry noticed a bottle floating near the rocks. We found a driftwood stick and fished the bottle close to the shore. We noticed a paper rolled up inside the bottle. Excitedly we ran to show the family what we found. Dad popped the cork and carefully fished the paper out of the bottle. *Wow*! It was a treasure map. It was a map of Turtle Island."

According to the brothers, the map had an "X" and a compass denoting north, south, east and west, along with details like "so many paces from this tree, in this direction," etc. They could see the island from the Grays' house and begged their parents to go find the treasure.

> *Uncle Bill's sailboat was anchored in front of the house. Mom and Dad said we could go. We grabbed a pick and a shovel that conveniently were leaning on the garage nearby. It was a beautiful, warm summer day with a lite wind. Turtle Island was about five miles northwest of the Grays' house. You can just imagine the excitement of three young boys in a sailboat following a dream. We were going to be rich.*
>
> *We beached the boat and jumped in water. We pulled the boat up on the sand.*

We looked at the map and started following the directions. The map appeared wrinkled and old. The edges were burned for authenticity.

Twenty-Five (three feet per pace) paces, here, fifteen paces to a large willow tree. An "X" marked the spot. Three wide-eyed little boys started digging.

We found the treasure chest. It was a couple feet long and a foot wide. The top was humped. The chest looked authentic—just like in the pirate movies. Uncle Bill broke the lock with a pickaxe. We were awestruck as we saw coins (plastic) and piles of costume jewelry. We were rich little boys. We took our riches and sailed back to Bill and Katie's house. Proudly, we showed our riches to our relatives that were there for the day.

It wasn't until years later that we realized we'd been had. We still have a good laugh at the ingenuity of our uncle Bill.

Christmas in a Lighthouse

Christmas Day 1919 wasn't a typical Christmas for Captain Chauncey Fitzmorris.

"There will be no one to greet him with a joyous 'Merry Christmas' this morning; there will be no Christmas carols ringing in his ears, no Yuletide packages to open and enjoy, nor even Christmas cards or letters to receive and read," says a 1919 *Wilmington News-Journal* article. That's because Captain Fitzmorris spent Christmas in the West Sister Island Lighthouse. He had been its guardian for twelve years, living on the ninety-acre Lake Erie Island located between Sandusky and Toledo. "His only companion is a 19-year-old nephew, and together the two are in voluntary exile—not to hear other human voices nor to receive mail or papers, nor to be in communication with the rest of the world until navigation opens on the Great Lakes next April, for they are the only two human beings on West Sister Island."

The captain took his last glimpse of the mainland and his friends and family the day before Thanksgiving, when he made his farewell trip to Port Clinton for supplies.

He was said to be the only lighthouse keeper on inland waters in America to spend the winter in such exile, since all other Great Lakes light keepers either went to the mainland when navigation closed in the fall or were stationed at lights in contact with the mainland.

As the lightkeeper, Captain Fitzmorris made several rescues, including those of the passengers of a small yacht that capsized nearby. "Captain

Fitzmorris chopped through the walls of the yachts cabin to rescue two women and a baby imprisoned there, and is said to have been recommended for a government medal for his valorous work," reads the article.

Yet the light's most intense island rescue involved Captain Fitzmorris himself. The previous winter, a relief party was organized by the life-saving guards at Marblehead because someone on Locust Point, the closest spot on the mainland, saw a distress light flashing from one of the West Sister tower windows. The guards battled through the choppy and icy waters for hours to reach the island, where they found Fitzmorris close to death from being gored by a bull. "His light had been flashed for two weeks before seen on the main land," says the article. "He was rushed to a hospital and immediately upon recovering insisted upon returning to his state of voluntary exile in his little stone dwelling in the base of the light tower."

Not even Captain Fitzmorris's wife could be convinced to stay on the island in the winter. After braving two years on the island, she decided to spend the winter of 1919 in Buffalo.

To survive the harsh conditions, Captain Fitzmorris was provided with government rations, a medical kit and fuel, but there was no way to know if he was well or even alive until navigation season reopened in April, "unless the stretch of land between Locust Point and the island freezes sufficiently to permit walking to the mainland."

But this was something the island loner seemed quite content with. "Fitzmorris says he likes the weird solitude of his isolation and enjoys the quietude of the island during the long winter months."

Detroit Boat Club

Detroit, Michigan, is ideally situated for water enthusiasts, alongside the Detroit River, which connects to Lake St. Clair to the north and Lake Erie to the south.

Boats regularly cruise these waterways, but many don't realize that from the late 1860s to early 1880s, the city was an epicenter for rowing.

According to Stephen Malbouef, an archivist and historian for the Detroit Boat Club (DBC) and Detroit Boat Club Crew (DBCC), there have been over seventy rowing clubs in Detroit, with close to thirty operating in 1879. "It was the most popular sport in the city," Stephen explained. "Some regattas would attract about a quarter to half of the city's population."

At the time, most of Detroit's large working-class population lived close to the riverfront, helping grow the sport's popularity. Detroit also lacked parks, so the river served as an opportunity to get out and exercise.

The Detroit Boat Club was founded as the city's first rowing club in 1839 and gradually became a social boating club, with competitive rowing, sailing, power boating, canoeing and swimming teams. The club's boathouse changed locations over the years. The first was constructed where the Renaissance Center is today. Then another boathouse was built at the foot of Rivard Street, and later, another was built at the foot of Hastings Street.

As the riverfront became more industrialized and more clubs were organized, a new boathouse district developed farther upriver, centered on Joseph Campau Avenue, where the DBC built a boathouse in 1873.

The DBC was one of the largest boat clubs in the United States in terms of membership size, number of boats and boathouse size. While most people think of rowing and sailing as sports for the wealthy—and the DBC did have some of Detroit's well-to-do citizens as members—most of the memberships of the rowing clubs on the river were made up of blue-collar workers, with groups of eight to ten people deciding to pool their money to buy a boat, becoming a club of their own.

Riverside view of boathouse, 1902. *Courtesy of Detroit Boat Club.*

"Two of the stove companies had their own boat club. The Detroit Stove Works had the Crown Jewel Boat Club, which was named after their popular stoves," Stephen said. "Downriver the iron workers of Detroit would form their clubs so they could race against the stove club."

By the 1880s, rowing was declining, and by 1893, the city had just two rowing clubs, down from nearly thirty a decade earlier. This was due to fewer people living near the river as access became choked off due to industrialization, the formation of Detroit's first professional baseball team in 1881 and an increase in recreational parkland.

The DBC's Belle Isle Boathouse, constructed in 1902, is the sole remaining historic rowing boathouse on the Detroit River. It was the club's seventh structure and the third to be built on Belle Isle. After the previous two boathouses burned down, the club decided to build a fireproof structure instead.

According to Stephen:

> *The result was the Venetian-Spanish revival building that we see today, which was constructed with solid brick load-bearing walls coated with white Portland cement stucco, reinforced concrete floors, steel columns and beam and a red Spanish tile roof. Like most Detroit boathouses of the era, the building is constructed over the river on pilings rather than on dry land. The boathouse's pilings are of wood and were driven twenty-eight feet deep into the riverbed. As they are in the riverbed and not exposed to oxygen, they will not rot.*

According to legend, the boat club wasn't built directly on Belle Isle so it could sell alcohol. Since alcohol wasn't allowed to be sold on Belle Isle, the club built its own island to become exempt.

"While an interesting story, it isn't true," said Stephen.

The DBC had banned alcohol in its boathouses since the 1870s and didn't officially start serving alcohol until after Prohibition to attract new members after experiencing a significant drop in membership during the Great Depression.

Considering the boathouse's location in the Detroit River, a key waterway for rumrunning during Prohibition, one may think the DBC was conveniently located to aid in the illegal transport of alcohol, but the only known connection was of a member who passed a story down to his son: "A guy who reached out a few years ago said his dad was a coxswain at the boat club during Prohibition. His dad told him the story in the '70s,

that his crew rowed went over to Canada and got a case of Canadian Club (whiskey) and then rowed it back to the Detroit side and sold it to a secret bar on the riverfront."

To maintain its membership numbers, the DBC increased the boathouse's dining room and kitchen space and provided dormitories for rowers, allowing them to train twice a day and sleep there overnight. When the Detroit Yacht Club opened its new facility in 1923, it was twice the size of the DBC boathouse and offered members parking and swimming pools. The DBC realized it needed to act fast to retain membership, so it added a fifty-meter Olympic distance swimming pool, allegedly the first such pool to be built by a private organization in the United States. It also added a children's wading pool and a large parking lot (the excavated dirt began filling out the island that would surround the boathouse).

In its prime, the boathouse's first floor housed the rowing and boating side of the club, with boat storage, a plunge bath and locker room. The second floor was the main social floor for men and women, with a lobby, dining room, ballroom and sitting rooms. The third floor, which was "men's only," housed the club's den, the original kitchen and some apartments. Only men could be members until the mid-1970s, when women were allowed to join. Prior, women could only have club privileges if their husbands were members or if they were the guest of a member. If her husband died, a

Opposite: A view of the Detroit River from the water. *Courtesy of Kelly Becay.*

Right: A view of Put-in-Bay from the water. *Courtesy of Kelly Becay*

woman could become a "Ladies Privilege" member, which allowed them to continue using the boathouse.

Since the boathouse was built with only a men's locker room, women simply changed into their bathing suits in their second-floor bathroom. However, as the sport's popularity increased, the board of directors, horrified by the sight of women walking through the formal spaces of the second floor in their bathing suits, quickly had a ladies locker room constructed on the first floor.

One of the DBC's largest annual events was its anniversary party, celebrating its founding on February 18, 1839. As early as the 1870s, the boat club hosted anniversary celebrations ranging from informal gatherings to elaborate ferry trips to Put-in-Bay. When the Belle Isle Boathouse opened, the club began holding its parties there. By the 1930s, the club started celebrating with a new tradition: an enormous cake.

"To give an example of the scale of these cakes, the 1934 iteration began construction—and I do mean construction—a month in advance so that there was enough time to bake and construct it in-house by the Detroit Boat Club kitchen staff, supervised by head baker William Wiesman," Stephen explained. The nine-layer fruitcake weighed 558 pounds and contained a gallon of rum and three-quarters of a gallon of brandy. "By 1936, the cake had grown to a 5-foot-tall, 15-layer fruitcake weighing in at 620 pounds,

A 1,100-pound cake created for the Detroit Boat Club's one hundredth anniversary. From the *Centennial Book of the Detroit Boat Club*, January 1940. *Courtesy of the Detroit Boat Club.*

with sugar decorations that included foot-high sailboats and oarsmen. The following year, the cake was 700 pounds, before finally, the largest cake of them all was created for the club's one hundredth anniversary celebration in 1939, weighing in at over half a ton, a whopping 1,100 pounds, with 100 candles to celebrate 100 years."

The oldest living member of the DBC cut the cake each year; the oldest members in the 1930s had been born in the 1840s and '50s.

According to Stephen:

> *Among the reasons given for why these cakes were so large was that since the birthday celebrations were typically member-only affairs (meaning no women present since membership was restricted to men at the time), the size of the cake allowed for members to take a slice home to their wives to prove their alibi that they were in fact at the DBC all night. The tradition of the birthday cakes sliced by the oldest living member continued through at least the 1950s and 1960s, although they eventually transitioned away from the hefty fruit cakes to more reasonable layered sheet cakes. None ever again rivaled the size and weight of the cakes in the 1930s.*

The club was at its peak from the 1920s through 1960s, with about 1,500 members. As Detroit's population decreased, so did the club's membership, dropping to just over 200 by the early 1990s. This forced the club into bankruptcy. The City of Detroit took ownership of the boathouse, leasing a portion to the DBC before evicting the club in favor of a new tenant, but this ended up falling through. When the DBC left the building, the rowers split off as a separate organization under Friends of Detroit Rowing (FODR), a nonprofit founded by DBC alumni rowers in 1972 to support rowing in Detroit. The city allowed the rowers to stay in the boathouse until it could figure out what to do with the building, and this lasted for eighteen years. In 2014, as part of Detroit's bankruptcy agreements, Belle Isle was leased to the State of Michigan as a state park. FODR then secured a thirty-year lease on the boathouse through the DNR, allowing it to have a more permanent position on Belle Isle and to rent the boathouse out for events. Volunteers spent hours putting hundreds of thousands of dollars, mainly donations and event rental revenue, which was required to go back into the building, into projects to stabilize, upgrade and restore the building. Renovations slowed when rentals couldn't take place during the COVID-19 pandemic. Just as FODR was preparing for a busy 2022 season, a portion of one of the club's porches collapsed, forcing the DNR to close the building.

Today, the DBC remains the oldest sailing club in the Americas, and the Detroit Boat Club Crew is the second-oldest rowing club in the Americas. The Belle Isle Boathouse is the last remaining historic rowing boathouse in Michigan and among the top twenty oldest rowing boathouses in the United States.

It has ties to industrial titans and history makers, like Henry Ford, who was once a member. The Henry Ford Museum has a photo of Ford and his board of directors on the front steps of the boathouse in 1908, less than two weeks before they released the Model T. Other distinguished guests included Detroit mayors, U.S. senators and congressmen and legendary aviatrix Amelia Earhart, who lectured on flying there in 1929.

Stephen is not only a historian, but he has also been an active rower with the FODR and Detroit Boat Club Crew for more than a decade. He received his bachelor's and master's degrees in architecture from the University of Detroit, and his master's thesis project investigated how the Belle Isle Boathouse could be renovated and restored to support a modern-day rowing program.

"As the first building everyone sees when they enter or leave the island, it's a historic landmark on Belle Isle. It's not as far gone as people were saying. It's got some issues with its exterior stucco and porches, but the majority of the building is solid," said Stephen.

Stephen, an architectural associate at InSite Consulting Architects in Madison, Wisconsin, which focuses on historic preservation, is working with a developer to renovate and restore the boathouse to include two restaurants, an event space, an indoor training space for the rowers and a reactivated marina, among other things. If his proposal is finalized, Stephen and his firm would be the architects working on the restoration, which would allow the beauty of the architecture and the history of Detroit rowing at the Belle Isle Boathouse to be preserved and enjoyed by future generations.

Hotel Lakeside: Nooks, Crannies and Legends

Melissa Ladd has always loved history. While growing up on Put-in-Bay and Catawba Island, she was surrounded by the region's unique maritime past. So it's no wonder that for four summers (2013 to 2017) during her undergraduate break from the College of Wooster, where she studied art history and archaeology, she was drawn to work as a housekeeper at Hotel Lakeside, one of the region's most legendary historic sites.

The hotel was built in 1875 and still stands in much of its original glory on the edge of Lake Erie in the gated community of Lakeside, Ohio. The community on the Marblehead Peninsula was created 150 years ago by a group of like-minded individuals who wanted to create a family-friendly retreat.

"The concept of Lakeside crystallized in part out of local Methodists' concerns about the flourishing wine industry on the nearby Lake Erie Islands," reads a 2023 *Echoes* magazine article by Kaysie M. Harrington. "Alcoholic beverages were viewed as a danger to families and a detriment to an individual's relationship with God." The alcohol-free resort offered respite.

"It was interesting to work behind the scenes of an old hotel that remarkably never burned or ever had any real adjustments made after the very early years," Melissa said. She explained the only major changes the hotel had to its exterior was the addition of the east wing, which added seventy rooms and was completed in 1890, and the removal of the second-floor balcony, which spanned the entire north side of the hotel looking over the water.

She said housekeeping was a lot of hard work, particularly because the historic hotel has many varied room layouts, but it was also a lot of fun, since so many of the other housekeepers were around her age. She remembers finding interesting cubbies, closets and historic items while exploring the building on slower workdays. Melissa admits the combination of her youth and the intrigue of the building led to a bit of rebellious activity. She and some of the other staff members sometimes went up to the roof to enjoy the scenic lakefront view, although they weren't technically supposed to.

She also once slept overnight in the linen closet (that was actually quite large) at the hotel in between work shifts after enjoying an evening of drinks with fellow hotel workers at the local watering hole Jamestown Tavern in Marblehead. She chose to walk back to the hotel instead of driving home. She made an interesting discovery in that linen closet in the downstairs hallway: a pulley system and a crate from the hotel's early days. "They would use it to raise and lower linens on a pulley system before there was an elevator so they wouldn't have to drag linens downstairs." She said the linen closet and pulley system are no longer there, having been used in the creation of an extra-large suite, but it must have been used for quite a while because the hotel didn't have an elevator installed until 1990.

While working at the hotel, Melissa said the hallway on the second floor was lined with smaller rooms that were built as staff and servant quarters, but in recent years, they, too, were combined during remodeling and the room doors were drywalled over.

"There's a staircase there that leads from the second floor straight down into the kitchen on the bottom floor, where the kitchen has always been. That stairwell has been signed, kind of like graffiti. There were people signing their names on the wall in the 1920s." The original signatures are still there; however, they were covered up with whitewash about a decade ago. Right after the names were painted over, hotel employees, including Melissa, began writing their names on the walls along the servant staircase once again.

Melissa said the housekeeping and kitchen staff supervisors told them not to use the stairwell to get to their office next to the kitchen on the bottom floor, likely due to the stairwell's diminishing structural integrity. "Of course, we always did anyway, since we were young and the convenience and discreetness of using them far outweighed any potential hazards in our minds. Looking back, I know why the administration wanted to keep us out; that stairwell, even today, has remained almost entirely untouched in many, many years," Melissa explained.

Melissa is now the archivist and operations manager of the Lakeside Heritage Society, working to preserve and share the community's unique history.

Published and Copyrighted 1884 by A. J. Hare, Sandusky, O.

76-694920

1. Hotel.
2. General Office.
3. English Auditorium.
4. German Auditorium.
5. Dining Halls.

SUMMER RESORT

LAKESI

Near SANDUSKY, OHI

Lakeside Summer Resort in 1884 (the hotel is the large building in the lower righthand corner). *Library of Congress.*

Left: Hotel Lakeside's servant stairwell. *Courtesy of Melissa Ladd.*

Opposite: A portrait of "Susan" in Hotel Lakeside. *Courtesy of Melissa Ladd.*

The Victorian-style hotel, with its wraparound porch, has been a haven for all kinds of visitors over the last century and a half—from those involved in the Chautauqua movement, a cultural and educational movement that flourished during the late nineteenth and early twentieth centuries, and has been a pivotal part of the community. It has hosted big names like President Rutherford B. Hayes, First Lady Eleanor Roosevelt, women's rights activist Susan B. Anthony and famed aviatrix Amelia Earhart.

Melissa said the Lakeside Heritage Society has various guest books from the hotel in its archive, including the one Hayes signed, which was on display at the hotel for years.

In preparation for the 150th anniversary of both the hotel and the Lakeside Heritage Society's museum, Heritage Hall (the original church of Lakeside), in 2025, Ladd began going through items that had been closed up for years in the Lakeside Association building's vault. In her search, she discovered a box with skeleton keys from Hotel Lakeside etched with the numbers of the original rooms. "We have a lot of hotel stuff, so it's cool to have the memory of working there in a much more contemporary time and then be in this position where we have a lot of artifacts from the hotel," she explained.

An interesting piece of hotel history hangs across from the stairway on the second floor: the image of a woman who, legend says, died while staying at the hotel. The portrait is simply signed, "Thorp, 1892."

Melissa said that while working at the hotel, she was sometimes asked about hotel hauntings, but she's a bit of a skeptic and never experienced anything like doors slamming or lights flickering. She did, however, hear local legends that may have sparked the ghost stories, likely changing and shifting through the years. One is about the woman in the picture, named Susan, who was prominent in Lakeside.

"What I had heard most was that this woman had committed suicide in the room—just the crazy stories that you hear. I don't know where that originated. In real life, that was not the case. There probably was in real life a woman who passed away in that room, but I don't have any historical documents. It may not have even happened at all," Melissa said.

Another possible tie involves Susan B. Anthony's visit in 1890, when she spoke at Central Auditorium (where Hoover Auditorium stands today). "Anthony's visit prompted a very inaccurate worldwide broadcast," reads Sheri Trusty's 2018 *Port Clinton News Herald* article. "'It was so hot, she fainted,' [Dakota] Harkins [then manager of operations at Lakeside] said. 'The AP got a hold of it and reported she died at Lakeside. Thankfully, she thought it was funny.'"

A view of Hotel Lakeside from a steamship. *Courtesy of the Lakeside Heritage Society.*

Melissa heard that newspapers quickly printed another story saying the story wasn't true. "She may have gotten woozy or collapsed here and they just brought her to her room to recover," Melissa explained. However, over the years, this misunderstanding could have evolved into the story of the Lakeside ghost.

According to Melissa, if anyone has, in fact, heard unusual noises while staying at the hotel, they may be linked to a furry culprit: racoons. She recalls that when she worked there, "so many raccoons get into the hotel in the winter, and every spring the maintenance crew goes on a full *Caddy Shack* adventure that is always hilarious." She said back then, raccoons lived in the ceiling in the winter, and in the spring, maintenance trapped and released them.

Of course, the noises may also just be attributed to the age of the building; 150 years is a long time to be a pillar in a community. The hotel has stood through the age of steamships, the Golden Age of industry, through wars and the Great Depression and the rise of new technology.

Hotel Lakeside stands as an important landmark that is still pivotal to the resort community, and everyone who has worked there, stayed there or lived nearby are all important pieces of its living history.

4
Unique Homes and Neighborhoods

Mari-Dor Beach Cottages

Mari-Dor Beach has been a haven of peace, quiet and nature for generations of visitors.

The current owner, Doug Kishman, is the fourth generation to own and operate the beloved Mari-Dor Beach on Lake Road between Vermilion and Huron, Ohio, along Lake Erie's shoreline. His great-grandfather Werner Kishman bought the property in 1861 after working in Vermilion as a blacksmith fitting out the iron work on ships being built there. "His goal was to buy and run a farm, so he saved his money and purchased the 45-acre Mari-Dor property, which had 880 feet of lakefront," Doug explained. "The north side of the farm, closest to the lake, was a fruit orchard, and the first summer people from towns like Lorain and Cleveland showed up and wanted to tent camp under the fruit trees. The cool summer lake breezes, the beach and fishing drew more and more people to vacation there."

Doug said his great-grandfather was an entrepreneur who saw the potential to make more money with his beautiful property, so he and his son A.J. built a few cottages—the first a converted chicken coop—as summer rentals. The rentals were popular, so they added more cottages through the 1920s and '30s.

In the 1930s, during the Great Depression, Mari-Dor become a brief respite for a few days for a couple who was traveling across the country with their five children on a self-made contraption of two bikes connected

This page, top: Mari-Dor Beach cottages, 1940s. *Author's collection.*

This page, bottom: Tent camping at Mari-Dor Beach, circa 1900. *Courtesy of the Kishman family.*

Opposite, top: A couple and their children traveling cross country with their bicycle rig stop to rest at Mari-Dor Beach, 1930s. *Courtesy of the Kishman family.*

Opposite, bottom: The entrance to Mari-Dor Beach in 1930s. *Courtesy of the Kishman family.*

MARI-DOR BEACH
MARI-DOR
ROYAL CROWN
BEACH
WELCOME
COTTAGE
NO
VACANCY

with a storage and seating space. "They were riding from the East Coast to resettle and look for opportunities in California. They didn't have money for a car, so they created this rig to get them there. We never did find out what happened to them. A bit of a *Grapes of Wrath* kind of deal."

"Mari-Dor," a hybrid of Doug's grandfather's daughters' names, Marion and Doris, was placed above the entrance to the general store and gas station, opened in the 1930s, and on the arched sign at the entrance to the resort. Over time, they realized the store didn't bring in much money, so they closed it and moved the building to the lakefront, transforming it into another summer cottage. By the 1940s, Mari-Dor had seventeen cottages and forty trailer spaces.

Doug said they have had many groups of regulars come and go through the years. "One of the best things about Mari-Dor is that whole extended families can—and have—come here to spend vacations together," he said. "Brothers, sisters, aunts and uncles and even friends that have met here and become like family during their stays. We've had couples meet, fall in love, and marry after meeting their spouse here at the beach. That included my mother, Betty Kishman, who married my father, Paul Kishman, after meeting here. They ran the cottages from the 1940s until I took over in the 1990s."

Doug has worked at Mari-Dor since he was a kid, even though he also had a career as a high school teacher. Now, the next generation of Kishmans are beginning to take over. "Along with my wife, my son and daughter's families,

Boats anchored off Mari-Dor Beach. *Courtesy of the Kishman family.*

we are still at it here, renting to many of the descendants of renters from years past. We have a couple families who are fourth and fifth generations' worth of summer renters, some going all the way back to the 1800s tent camping days."

The family's success for more than 165 summers is a testament to their dedication to each other and their guests, creating a family vacation tradition on the shores of Lake Erie that brings generations of guests back again and again.

Thank you to local history enthusiast Dan Brady, of Brady's Bunch of Lorain County Nostalgia, *for sharing his knowledge of Mari-Dor and connecting this author with Doug.*

Presque Isle Houseboats

Houseboats on Horseshoe Pond, in Erie's Presque Isle, are a unique part of the region's local history.

According to Eugene Ware's 2020 GoErie article, settlers of Slovak and Russian descent built the first houseboats in Erie around 1890. "Most of the houseboats were built and owned by people who could not afford traditional homes. Many others soon joined them, and a colony of houseboats began to spread all over Presque Isle Bay. Most of them were moored along the Presque Isle shoreline," the article reads.

At the time, there weren't any specifications for building the houseboats or mooring them. "At one point, Joe Root, that old hermit who lived on Presque Isle, said that some of his shacks on the park were in better shape than many of the first houseboats. Joe always told Erie citizens that they were friendly people who loved their life on the water as squatters," Ware wrote.

The dilapidated houseboats were spread all over the bay, and it was common to hear fights occurring between owners, so by the late 1930s, standards of construction and placement were set for the houseboats and the Park and Harbor Commission was given control of all water inland and within five thousand feet of Presque Isle. Ware wrote,

> *They also gave the power to set minimum standards for all boats within this control zone. The final requirement under the new law was that all houseboats were to be moved to Misery Bay. Many of the houseboats never made the move as the owner could not meet the new commonwealth*

Houseboats in Horseshoe Pond. *Photo by Tim McLaughlin.*

> *standards. This was true because many were built before 1921, and most were more than 20 years old. Another interesting fact is that allowing these homes on a state park is very unusual. Normally, people are not allowed to live in a state park. This feature was grandfathered into the legislation at the time.*

The U.S. Coast Guard dug a channel from Misery Bay to Horseshoe Pond in the 1950s, and twenty-four of the twenty-nine to thirty-six houseboats that were on Misery Bay made the move to Horseshoe Pond. Once there, owners leased a renewable space for a decade, chose between several types of anchors and flotation that could be used in the pond and connected to electricity that reached the houseboats through a buried electrical line on the bottom of the pond.

"Houseboats have become increasingly popular," reads a 1960 advertisement in Erie, Pennsylvania's *Lake Shore Visitor.* "Most of these craft combine compact living quarters and a practically unsinkable hull. While speed is not one of the features of these boats, lots of fun is!" The advertisement shared the dimensions and 1960s cost of a houseboat: twenty-five by eight feet was the smallest footprint, and it could sleep four. It was advertised as having a gas stove, refrigerator, toilet, kitchen and dining area, and it could be purchased for $1,500 to $2,000, while the larger houseboats could cost $5,000.

House with a View and a Speakeasy

Blind pig, gin joint, speakeasy—whatever you call it, they were rampant during Prohibition. Between 1920 and 1933, people across the United States tried to skirt around the law preventing the sale, importation and exportation of alcohol, risking thousands of dollars in fines if caught.

Some businesses had secret doors and passwords to get into hidden bars where booze was served, while some homes, particularly along Lake Erie, had their own speakeasies tucked into back rooms and basements. Rumrunning liquor between Canada and the United States was big business since it was legal to produce alcohol in Canada, and points along the Lake Erie shoreline became drop-off and pick-up sites.

In between Edgewater Park and Lakewood Park in Cleveland sits a 1920s home that was believed to have housed a speakeasy. The nearly eight-thousand-square-foot house, built in 1924 at 11415 Harborview Avenue, had an ideal location for rumrunning across the street from Lake Erie.

Dorothy Mlakar Bianchi, a longtime family friend who grew up next door to this author's mother, Joanne (Perusek) Boresz, and aunt Peggy (Perusek) Zirbes in Euclid, Ohio, shared the story of her connection to the Harborview House with my mom and me, knowing it could be a perfect fit for one of my books. It used to belong to her uncle Frank and aunt Sophie Laurich, who bought the house after the 1930s stock market crash and lived there with their two children. Dorothy fondly remembers visiting the home with her parents, Ann and Anthony Mlakar, throughout her childhood and exploring its nooks and crannies with her cousins.

"They let us do whatever we wanted," Dorothy recalled. "They let us run around, and off the kitchen there were spiral stairs that went all the way to the top floor that the maids and servants once used, so we found all of that fascinating."

She remembers a ballroom on the top floor and unique details like little windows on the exterior doors. "There were those small hatch windows. If you were inside, you just took the little knob and opened it. There was grating on it so you could see who was there, like a typical speakeasy."

As a child, Dorothy thought it was just a fun little feature, but years later, in 2001, her husband, John, was reading the *Plain Dealer* and came across an article titled "1920s Lake-View House Comes Complete with a Speakeasy." "And he said, 'Hey—this is your aunt and uncle's house!'" remembered Bianchi. She had no idea until reading that article that her family's home was an active gathering place during Prohibition.

The article by Shari M. Sweeney states that in 2001, the home's main entrance was at the side beneath a porte-cochere, "through which the concrete driveway winds to a carriage house/garage. What appears to be the front entrance—leaded glass doors, curved terrace, wrought-iron fence—is actually a smoking terrace off the living room to which male guests once retired for after-dinner cigars." A wide center staircase sits in the entry hall, along with a massive wood-burning fireplace and floor-to-ceiling windows with a view of Lake Erie.

"Arguably the most interesting feature of this house, though, is an area that has remained largely untouched: Lotty's Pub, an honest-to-goodness speakeasy in the basement." That name was carved into a small wooden sign that was hanging at the bottom of the stairs.

The *Plain Dealer* article goes on to say:

> *A vault now used as pantry space was intended to hold illegal shipments of liquor during Prohibition. The trapdoor in the vault floor opened to a tunnel directly accessing the lake, across the street.*
>
> *Other evidence of speakeasy activity includes an 80-year-old intercom system and tiny "shutters"—precursors to peepholes, perhaps—on heavy wood exterior doors.*

There were a couple of ways to get down into the basement, different staircases—one off the kitchen and one off the hallway, underneath the stair.

Dorothy remembers her uncle showing her the vault when she was an adult but never knew about the tunnel or its role as a speakeasy, and she believes he was unaware of it, too. "If he knew it was there, he never told me," explained Dorothy. "The vault was down in the basement, and he took me down there and said that it was a walk-in safe." She said the vault was about eight by ten feet, and the room around the corner from it had a bar in the corner and a pool table. After walking up a step, there was a fireplace and intimate seating area. She assumes that is where the speakeasy was. "So, the booze would come in and then go around the corner to the bar. Back during Prohibition, it probably was to hold liquor when they brought it in—that was where that trapdoor was. If they knew, they didn't talk about it."

However, Dorothy had another aunt and uncle, Jennie (Laurich) and Joseph Schultz, who lived in the old carriage house for a while. They became friendly with the neighbors, who told them there used to be many parties at the house prior to her aunt and uncle owning it, with glamorous women and men regularly going in and out. Bianchi also heard the woman who originally built the house came from Florida and insisted that the home be built to withstand a hurricane. Builders tried to assure her that she wasn't at risk of hurricanes living near Lake Erie, but as the story goes, she insisted.

Over the century or so since the house was built, many details have changed throughout it. Dorothy's aunt replaced the Tiffany lampshades that hung over the dining room table with light fixtures that were more her style. The couple who owned it at the time the 2001 article was written, David and Trisha Campbell, converted the third-floor ballroom into a media room and bedrooms with window seats to accommodate their large family of eight children. And previous owners had transformed a sitting room off the master bedroom into a spacious bath and walk-in closet.

The current owners, Robert and Brenda Rose, bought the home in 2011. Robert said the realtor told them about the house's speakeasy-related features and the bank vault in the basement. As for the tunnel that led from that vault to an unknown spot across the street, not much of it remains to be seen. "There's a metal plate over a hole in the floor, and the hole in the floor was filled in with concrete block," according to Robert.

It's unknown where the tunnel may have led to since the homes that currently stand across the street were built in the 1950s. Perhaps there was an entry point on the lakefront cliff that has since been sealed or collapsed—or maybe it's just hidden, waiting to be rediscovered.

5
Celebrations and Recreation

Cranberry Day

Most people enjoy celebrating holidays and birthdays, but at one time on Presque Isle, in Erie, an abundant harvest of a small berry was met with just as much excitement.

In the mid-1800s, wild cranberries grew along the swampy interior sections of the peninsula. According to the 1896 *Nelson's Biographical Dictionary and Historical Reference Book of Erie County*:

> *The protection of* [cranberries] *was carefully looked after. An Act of Assembly imposed a fine of not less than ten dollars, nor more than twenty-five dollars, on any person who should gather cranberries between July and October. The first Tuesday of October was "Cranberry Day," a great event in olden times.*

Boatloads of people crossed the bay at night and stayed until the morning, picking berries and partying, according to Becky Weiser on the Hagan History Center's site. The $10 to $25 fine for picking berries before harvest season began would be equivalent to about $300 to $750 today. By 1900, the cranberries were being depleted and eventually stopped growing.

Weiser's grandmother Agnes (Lucas) Weigert moved to Erie from Croatia when she was three years old. She made a beloved cranberry relish, which you can now make in honor of the region's long-ago ties.

Grandma Weigert's Cranberry Relish

1 whole orange
1 apple
1 pound cranberries
¼ cup chopped nuts (optional)
1 cup sugar
1 package raspberry Jell-O
1 cup boiling water
½ cup juice from cranberries, etc.

Grind together the orange, apple, fresh cranberries and nuts (use a Griswold grinder if you have one).

Mix in the sugar. Cover and let stand for two hours or more to draw out the juice.

Prepare the Jell-O, using one cup of boiling water and half a cup of the juice. (Discard or drink the rest.)

Let it set slightly.

Stir in the cranberry mixture and pour into a mold or into individual molds.

Finish setting.

Catawba Island: Boats, Barrels and Bottles

Fishing

Fishermen have lined the shores of Lake Erie for centuries and cast their lines from boats. The shallow, warm water of the western basin, including Sandusky, Marblehead, Lakeside and the islands, is known for being plentiful with fish.

"For many years, fishing in Lake Erie was done by individual families to supplement their own food supply, but in 1840, Henry Ellithorp discovered large quantities of fine white fish near the bass islands, and commercial fishing quickly became a profitable industry employing many men," according to the Catawba Island Township website. "Tons of fish were caught daily and shipped to markets around the country. The fishing

A man known as "Grandpa Hudek" with his fishing catch in Marblehead, Ohio. *Courtesy of Suzanne Reichert (Hudek's great-great-granddaughter).*

industry flourished for more than a century but went into a swift and nearly final decline in the 1950s."

Several reasons for the decline include overfishing, poor water quality and strict regulations, but other recreational and industrial booms helped gain Catawba recognition.

Quarry and Kiln

"For a short time between 1850 and 1860 large capital was interested in a cement project. Quarries were opened and a kiln erected, but the venture failed," according to the book *Legends of Catawba*, edited by Don Rhodes.

The book goes on to say that during the quarry's short heyday, hundreds of kiln and quarry workers populated Catawba Island. Hundreds of barrels and sacks of cement were loaded on lake freighters each day. "Never before had the island witnessed such activity."

A large supply store stood near the docks, run by a man known for having questionable business ethics. "Such for instance as his offer to the directors of the lime kiln to manage the work at about two hundred a year less than was paid to the then acting manager," reads *Legends of Catawba*. "His offer was accepted, and from its acceptance dated the decline in prosperity. His first act was to force his workers to accept in lieu of pay, an order on his store. Thus, he secured their undivided patronage."

The workers who refused were fired, and new workers were hired, even if they weren't efficient—which later showed in their work. His mismanagement led to "unruly" barrel makers in the cooperage shop, which started a trickle-down effect. "The barrels were so poorly constructed that hundreds of them fell apart as they were rolled down the wharf into the waiting boats. The cement too, was of a grade so inferior as to make it practically valueless. The result, of course, was the cancellation of contracts and the eventual shut-down. The workers left the island the former prosperity came to an end—the bubble had burst and the boom was over."

Around the same time, another industry was quickly developing that quite literally allowed Catawba Island to make a name for itself.

Wine

Vineyards and apple and peach orchards were developed commercially on several Lake Erie islands and Catawba Island (which is actually a peninsula).

"The island has at one time or another been part of four counties and as many townships," reads *Legends of Catawba*. "It was not until about 1860 that it received the name of Catawba from the grape of the same name that was introduced there at the time."

Catawba Island Wine Company, 1911. *Courtesy of Gideon Owen Wine Company.*

Catawba grapevines were brought up from North Carolina, and apples and peaches were shipped out via boat and railway in large quantities.

In the 1870s, a group of local farmers and grape growers formed the Catawba Island Wine Company. They built a winery that, although it has changed hands and names several times, still exists as Gideon Owen Wine Company on East Wine Cellar Road. According to the company's website, the 1872 construction included the tirage, ballroom, loft and four wine cellar vaults (that are still used). However, the company went bankrupt in the early 1900s, which left the building vacant for more than two decades.

In the 1920s, a renter from Detroit even used the building to house an indoor putt-putt course and tearoom, but by the late 1930s, it went back to its roots when it was sold to Mon Ami Champagne Company, a Texas-based

Left, top: Women at Mon Ami Champagne Company, 1937–40. *Courtesy of the Gideon Owen Wine Company.*

Left, bottom: Bottling at Mon Ami Champagne Company, 1937–40. *Courtesy of the Gideon Owen Wine Company.*

Opposite: Victor Von Baden (*center*), the president of Mon Ami Champagne Company. *Courtesy of the Gideon Owen Wine Company.*

company that relocated to Sandusky. "Mon Ami converted the building back into a winery and used it for the production and storage of champagne," the Gideon Owen Wine Company's website reads.

In 1940, the winery was thrust into the spotlight when Mon Ami's president, Victor Von Baden, was arrested and found guilty of tax evasion. Enrique M. Portales, director of marketing and information technology at Gideon Owen Wine Company, shared the story with me along with clippings from the *Port Clinton News Herald* archive.

The winery first made headlines in March 1940 in a *Port Clinton News Herald* article that stated, "Reports that the Mon Ami Champagne Company here had been raided and closed by federal authorities were denied Saturday." Von Baden told the *Herald* that agents from the internal revenue department's tax unit were just making a routine check at the winery because his company had applied for tax credit on one thousand bottles of wine. "He said that this number of bottles had been broken or destroyed during the year 1939, and that following appreciation for the credit the tax unit always make a check."

However, by October 1940, Von Baden was in Toledo's federal court, facing twenty-three counts of violating the federal wine tax laws.

The *Herald* reported:

> *On the witness stand, Von Baden said that in 1937 and 1938 more than 100 cases of various kinds of beverages had been returned to the winery by customers for a variety of reasons. Sometimes the customers credit was not good; the customer's had gone into receivership, and sometimes because the champagne was "wild" and therefore unsalable. All of this wine had the federal tax paid on it when first shipped, Von Baden told the court, and when it was returned, that which was saleable was offered for sale again without payment of further tax. He said undoubtedly some of this was re-shipped and when this was the case no new tax stamps were affixed.*

Von Baden was found guilty, sentenced to two and a half years in prison and fined $1,500 for violating the alcohol tax laws.

By early January 1941, Von Baden was taken from the Lucas County Jail to the Toledo federal courtroom, where he was held, along with his associates Willie Post and John G. Wagner, on new charges. It was alleged they had transferred wine stock illegally from the former Sandusky Wineries, Inc. from Sandusky to the Mon Ami firm on Catawba Island by failing to affix wine stamps to wine containers.

By the end of January 1941, the *Herald* reported that Von Baden had been sentenced to more than four years in prison for conspiracy and violating federal alcohol laws.

Then in 1943, a fire decimated the Mon Ami Champagne Company building, killing one worker and leaving only the original stone walls and four cellars intact. The estimated $24,000 loss in wine stocks was another heavy blow for the winery.

A few years later, the building was reconstructed and expanded to include a restaurant; the main floor (now the ballroom) was converted into dining space, and a kitchen was added on to the side (now known as the vineyard room).

According to the Gideon Owen Wine Company's website, the Mon Ami Champagne Co. name remained, although ownership changed hands from the Mantey family in the 1950s to Paramount Distilleries in 1980s. "Wine and champagne production ceased on-site and was moved to Meier's Wine Cellars and the Mantey Winery," reads the company's website. "But the lower cellar vaults were still used for storage. Around this time Mon Ami (under Paramount) ranked among the leading wineries in Ohio, producing 42,000–50,000 gallons of champagne annually."

By the mid-1980s, the building, no longer used for champagne storage, housed a restaurant and entertainment facility. An addition was built so the kitchen could span the back section of the building, and the old kitchen was remodeled into a tasting room and wine shop.

Then from 2001 to 2019, the building was purchased by an owner with ties to Firelands Winery, and nearly all of Mon Ami's wines were made off-site from grapes from all around the country.

In 2019, Quintin and Donna Smith bought the historic building and property with plans to preserve the site, plant vineyards and bring back winemaking to Catawba. The winery reopened in 2020 as Gideon Owen Wine Company, a name the Smiths chose to honor the island's early winemaking roots. A man named Gideon Stiles Owen opened a commercial winery on Northeast Catawba Road in 1865 "in a simple, tall wooden barn built over a stone cellar with an arched ceiling," according to the Catawba Island Historical Society. "Remains of the cellar can still be seen in a copse of trees across from the exit driveway of Twin Oast Brewing."

Owen's business was successful at first, but as the twentieth century approached, orchards began replacing Catawba's grape arbors. "Fortunately, Owen was an astute businessman and adapted well to the times. He converted the winery to a peach packing house and used excess fruit to distill brandy."

The Smiths wanted to recognize Owen for his contributions, since he is often forgotten when compared to the owners of larger area wineries of his time.

Two years after the new Gideon Owen Wine Company opened, it began crafting wines on site again, using the lower cellar and adjacent wine barn for production. "The winery's first vintage, made from Lake Erie AVA-grown grapes and produced entirely on-site in over 40 years, included a 2022 Chardonel, 2022 Pinot Grigio, 2020 Red Blend, 2022 Riesling, and a 2022 Rose of Cabernet Franc, all of which were released throughout 2023," the Gideon Owen Wine Company's website reads. "This marked a significant milestone in the winery's history and a testament to the Smiths' commitment to preserving the winery's legacy while also embracing the future of winemaking on Catawba Island."

Last Boat of the Season

Fireworks explode in the sky above Lake Erie's western basin, reflecting in the rippling water below, as a band plays on South Bass Island. Islanders gather around, chatting and enjoying hot dogs and cold drinks. This evening marks the unofficial close of summer on Put-in-Bay, an island sometimes called the "Key West of the north," and it is both bittersweet and celebratory.

There's even a song about it called "Waves," by Ray Fogg:

> *Well, it happens here every year. It's island tradition. On Labor Day, at 10 to 8, at the end of the season. To the Lime Kiln Dock, you will see them flock, all of the island people gather and the Miller Line passes out the wine as the dock hands start to scatter. The boat sounds its horn, then it pulls away. It turns to face the island. People on the coast, they raise a toast, here's to next year and they give a cheer and wave. They wave the summer away.*

This tradition started back in the 1990s, according to author and Lake Erie islands historian Michael Gora. He said that some claim that it restarted and continued a tradition that began when steamships, from Cleveland and Detroit, served the islands and publicized their "last boats of the season."

"The story is that the tradition started and ended originally with the steamer *Put-in-Bay* that made the run from Detroit and ran from 1911–1950. She docked at Fox's Dock in PIB harbor and not at Lime Kiln and ended her season on Labor Day," said Michael.

According to Katrina M. Reed with the Miller Ferry, after the line's official schedule ends, the Miller Ferry runs an extended schedule, and then after that ends, they occasionally run ferries as weather allows.

The Miller Ferry Line has been a part of the region's history for more than a century.

"We were founded in 1905 as a fishing charter and water taxi service in the summer and ice harvesting business in the winter," Katrina explained. According to the Miller Ferries site, the line then began ferry services in the 1940s. It goes on to say, "Miller Boat Livery became incorporated in 1966 and renamed Miller Boat Line. A breakwall along with a steel and concrete dock were added to Miller's Lime Kiln Dock on the southeast tip of Put-in-Bay." Michael Gora added, "Another last boat of the season that is sometimes publicized is the last fuel boat going to Put-in-Bay before the start of the winter."

A Banquet Fit for a Sewer

The words *banquet* and *sewer* don't typically go together. However, in 1906, when the Oakdale sewer in East Toledo was shiny and new, the men who built it enjoyed a feast *inside* of it.

According to the East Toledo Historical Society, *Sun Newspaper* shared the story in the *Sun*'s 25th Anniversary and East Side Historical issue:

> *What was probably the most unique and oddly located banquet ever held in Toledo—and perhaps anywhere, for that matter—was the celebration feast held on Monday, April 18, 1906, in the just completed new Oakdale sewer, which was to serve the people of the Oakdale section and South East Toledo.*

The banquet was meant to be the culmination of a sewer inspection trip that started at East Broadway and went west toward the Fassett Street Bridge. It was attended by a group of nineteen men, including the city engineer Frank Consaul, the president of the Board of Public Safety and inspectors who "donned old clothes, pulled on hip rubber boots, and clambered down the manhole at the point above named and crouched through the narrow part of the sewer for about an eight of a mile with stooped shoulders—and aching bones—guided only by the rays from two or three lanterns until they reached the point where the sewer got larger and they could walk erect."

According to the *Sun Newspaper* article, as they waded through the sewer water, Consaul pointed out design features to the other men, but they soon became distracted by a surprising smell, "the delicious odor of coffee permeating the damp atmosphere, and when they reached the spot the curtain was drawn aside and before them was spread the banquet table." The banquet included "blue points, radishes, young onions, celery, combination salad, hot stuffed tomatoes, potato salad, Waukesha Beer, coffee, cigars."

The men sat down at a candle-lit table, listened to congratulatory speeches and dined in (sort of) luxury in their rough clothes and rubber boots as sewer water swirled around their feet.

It has gone down in history as one of the least-known but most unique "waterfront" meals along Lake Erie.

WALDAMEER AMUSEMENT PARK

You can hear the roar of the rides at Waldameer Amusement Park before you even walk in. The sounds waft into the parking lot, encouraging visitors to come in and enjoy a day of fun.

I have been visiting Waldameer for decades—as an Erie reporter covering events there; as an aunt, visiting with my mom and niece; and now as a mom, visiting with my husband and kids. A visit to Waldameer is a much-requested summertime family trip. Everyone in my family has a different ride or section of the park they love, and of course, we always need to take a picture on the bench with Charlie the Waldameer clown (named after longtime Waldameer gardener Charlie Cox, according to a *Lake Erie Living* article by Kara Murphy).

Years ago, before Waldameer was even an amusement park, beckoning to thrill-seekers, it started out as a quiet picnic spot and bathing beach called Hoffman's Grove. Then, according to the park's website, in 1896, the Erie Electric Motor Company trolley line bought the property and renamed it Waldameer, which is German for "woods by the sea."

"The picnic area was highlighted by a large beach on Lake Erie and a modern bathhouse for the time. Some of the first 'rides' were along the lake shore," reads the park's website. "The trolley company expanded the

The walk from the beach to Waldameer Park, 1920s. *Author's collection.*

park with a $1,000 dance hall, carousel, and Hofbrau German beer garden complete with singing waiters in 1900."

If you visit the arcade at Waldameer today, you'll be standing on the site of the park's first roller coaster, the Figure 8 and Dip the Dips, which thrilled park-goers from 1902 to 1937. However, the ride was very tame by today's standards—it's largest drop was only nine feet, and it could go up to only ten miles per hour.

Even as more rides started popping up in the 1920s, like the miniature train, Caterpillar, funhouse, Whip and Old Mill, the park was still known as an ideal picnic locale. It was a popular spot for company picnics and school visits.

In November 1929, Cathedral School seventh grader Jack Corboy wrote in Erie's *Lake Shore Visitor* about his visit with his classmates to Waldameer in the fall:

> *Gathering nuts—walnuts and butternuts; eating hot wiener rolls and Kuneman's light, fluffy, sugared doughnuts; drinking piping hot coffee rich with cream, the Cathedral junior choir enjoyed a fall outing at Waldameer Saturday as the guests of the Rev. Gerald G. Dugan, rector of St. Peter's Cathedral.*
>
> *Gannon and Carey's truck conveyed the boys and girls to the park at 11:30 a.m. Perfect fall weather was in evidence. The sun shone bright and clear, the air was crisp and bracing. So much did the children enjoy the hiking that when 5 o'clock came and it was time to return home, they decided to hike right into town.*
>
> *Ann-Jane Dugan Monahan was our distinguished little visitor. She attempted to do everything that we did. Her pockets, too, bulged with nuts. When she waved goodbye to us as she was being driven off homeward, she looked as happy as we felt for our perfect and never-to-be-forgotten day.*

A May 16, 1930 "school news" article in the *Lake Shore Visitor* recounts a visit the junior choir of St. Peter's Cathedral made to the park:

> *We left the Villa Maria campus at 11 a.m. One of the boys started the day off right by breaking a window in the sun parlor at the Villa. The truck which conveyed us both ways was kindly donated by Mr. J.E. Gannon. He also furnished the candy.*
>
> *The picnic lunch which was served was very good. It consisted of sandwiches, cake, ice cream and ginger ale.*

Park tourist boats in lagoon at Waldameer, 1920s. *Author's collection.*

> *On arriving at Waldameer we went to the beach. Some of us went rowing in one of the ponds and others went swimming. In the afternoon we had a wading contest. The water was cool but refreshing. The girls did the tamer things, such as picking flowers.*

Waldameer remains the fifth-oldest continuously operating amusement park in the country and one of the most popular recreation sites along Lake Erie.

Old Cedar Point Road

I remember sitting down in the front seat and pulling the metal lever across my lap. My heart was racing with excitement.

I was fifteen years old, about to ride my first roller coaster with one of my best friends, Adrian (Hayden) Shaw, and I picked the front seat of the Magnum XL-200. Nearly a decade before, it had been the tallest roller coaster in the world when it opened at Cedar Point in 1989. Go big or go home.

We were fastened in, and the coaster started its suspensefully slow *clickety clack* (you know the exact sound I'm talking about if you've ridden it) ascent

Above: This author (*center*) with her dad (Dale Boresz, *right*) and friend Adrian (Hayden) Shaw (*left*) on Cedar Point beach, 1996. *Author's collection.*

Right: This author (*center*) with her mom (Joanne Boresz, *right*) and friend Adrian (Hayden) Shaw (*left*) on the sidewalk in between Hotel Breakers and Cedar Point Beach, 1996. *Author's collection.*

up the humongous hill. I was mesmerized by the spectacular view of the park and Lake Erie, suspended in a moment of beauty and calm at the top of the hill—until we were teetering, seemingly without gravity, before we plummeted face-first down a narrow precipice of tracks.

It was thrilling, and after that ride, I was hooked. My parents, Joanne and Dale Boresz, brought us to the park and patiently waited as we rode coaster after coaster well into the evening, when the view from the top of the rides at dusk became more magical as the sunset stretched out above the lake and the lights popped on in the park below.

This is the Cedar Point that has been drawing visitors for more than a century. Of course, it didn't start out with all the excitement it had for a teenager in the '90s or the expansive park it has grown into today. According to the park's website, Cedar Point opened in 1870 as a simple public bathing beach that visitors traveled to by steamship. The enormous Grand Pavilion opened in 1888, and the park's first roller coaster, the Switchback Railway, opened in 1892. By 1905, the historic Hotel Breakers, which is still operating today, welcomed its first guests (with six hundred rooms, it was one of the largest hotels in the Midwest). Two years later, the steamer *Eastland* (which later became the epicenter of the worst shipwreck on the Great Lakes when it overturned in Chicago) began transporting passengers back and forth between Cedar Point and Cleveland.

Cedar Point's rides, midway and long stretch of sand drew attention from all over. Even aviation great Glenn H. Curtiss set a world record here for

Cedar Point boat landing and dock, 1906. *Author's collection.*

flying over water in 1910 when he completed a sixty-five-mile-long flight from Euclid Beach to Cedar Point Beach.

More and more people wanted to see what this fun peninsula was all about, but it wasn't easy to get to. So, a new steamship service was started to help visitors get to the point without going through Port Clinton. "A service that will permit the residents of the peninsula to come to Sandusky and do their shopping as well as enjoy the pleasures that a visit at Cedar Point affords, will be inaugurated by the Toledo, Port Clinton & Lakeside Electric Ry. Co., July 1st," reads a 1911 article in the *Sandusky Register.*

Steamships were a popular form of transportation until the rise of the automobile. In 1911, according to Cedar Point's website, "Cedar Point announced that a roadway would be built to the resort, connecting it with the main arteries coming into the Sandusky area."

George A. Boeckling, who managed Cedar Point through one of its greatest periods of growth, from 1897 to 1931, saw the potential to build a road that would connect the park with the main roads coming into nearby Sandusky, according to the blog *Midwest Guest.* And he began work on the new road in 1913.

"The project was costly and difficult because it entailed construction through bog and marshland, but Boeckling knew that building the road would be an important factor in ensuring Cedar Point's future growth and success," wrote Dominique King on the blog *Midwest Guest.*

The automobile entrance to Cedar Point. *Author's collection.*

Cedar Point's auto road. *Author's collection.*

The two-lane highway, which opened in the summer of 1914 and ran one mile north to Lake Erie and then turned west for another six miles along the peninsula and into the park, became one of the first concrete roads in Ohio and was considered a great feat of engineering. It was named the Cedar Point Chaussee (French for "paved road") and was marked by a wrought-iron gate entrance.

And where there's roads, there's speeders. A 1919 *Sandusky Register* article reported Deputy Sheriff Englert arrested a Wisconsin man for fast and reckless driving. "He deposited a bond of $15 for his appearance this morning in Justice Merriam's court," reads the 1919 article. "Deputy Englert says that Phillips disregarded the rights of other autoists on the road and passed them at 45 miles. He narrowly missed forcing some cars into ditches along the road he claims. Deputy Englert has now mastered the motorcycles he rides and is prepared to wage war on all speeders and reckless drivers."

Within a few years of the road opening, several big storms washed out parts of it and caused damage to the eastern end. The original entrance was abandoned, and the road was rebuilt, with an entrance set two miles to the west at Cleveland Road, which shortened the drive to Cedar Point.

Steamship service to the park discontinued in 1952, and Cedar Point constructed the causeway into the park in 1957 to alleviate the traffic congestion along the Chaussee. This has become the park's main entrance, although some still enjoy a scenic ride along Cedar Point Road, lined with beautifully landscaped lakefront homes and an open view of Lake Erie.

My mother-in-law, Mary Ann (Babic) Engelking, remembers the long drive from Cleveland to Cedar Point that she took with her family in the early 1960s, before Interstate 90 was constructed. "As a little kid it felt like it took all day to get there," she recalled. "Then coming home I'd fall asleep in the back."

She remembers going to the park each year for her uncle Andy Babic's company picnic. She rode in the family station wagon—with no seatbelts, she added—with her mom and dad, Mary and Tony Babic, and her siblings. It was a big deal because not only did they not have to pay admission, but she also knew she had a fun day ahead and looked forward to it each year.

"My mom didn't like roller coasters or fast rides, but I didn't care; I just loved being there," she said. "One of our favorites was riding the old-fashioned cars and she'd let me sit in the driver's seat so I could 'drive.' I thought I was so grown up. Fun memory."

My mother-in-law also remembers going on Shoot the Rapids, and she loved the bumper cars. "Even though I was afraid to ride the coasters, I liked to stand close by and watch, especially if one of my siblings or cousins were on. It was thrilling to watch."

Today, that drive to Cedar Point is much faster, and although the original Cedar Point Road was removed, you can still find the ornate wrought-iron gate and brick pillars that once marked the road's majestic entrance. It's located at the entrance to the Sheldon Marsh State Nature Preserve, marked with a plaque designating it as a historic roadway, and that original part of the road is now a paved walking path that allows visitors to take a step back in time as they meander through the park.

Oldest and Longest Lakefront Pavilion on the Great Lakes

The 440-foot-long Lakeshore Park Main Pavilion, now known as the Ashtabula Township Park Lakefront Pavilion, is believed to be the longest and oldest lakefront pavilion on the Great Lakes.

It was designed by W.J. Kunkle and was created with a basement underneath to allow the public to have a picnic place, according to Carl E.

The beach and pavilion at Lake Shore Park in Ashtabula, Ohio, 1930–45. *Author's collection.*

Feather's book *Ashtabula Harbor, Ohio: A History of the World's Greatest Iron Ore Receiving Port.*

A 2004 Ohio Historical Marker at the site reads:

> *Built in 1919, the pavilion, with its bandstand/gazebo in the middle, is of steel frame construction, and stood unchanged for the most part except for the swept wing design roof replacement. Extensive Civilian Conservation Corps improvements were made in the park near the pavilion during the Great Depression of the 1930s. Since its founding, people from all over northeast Ohio, western Pennsylvania, and northern West Virginia have chosen this site for family outings and company, union, and political gatherings.*

The $40,000 pavilion was furnished with seats, tables and swings. According to Feather, "Floodlights were installed at the top of the building 'to make bathing even more pleasant in the evening than the daylight.'"

In 1921, visitors had a specific dress code for the bathing beach. Ladies couldn't wear a suit that "exposes the chest lower than a line drawn on a level with the arm pits," and blouse and bloomer suits could be worn as long as the blouse had one-quarter sleeves or close-fitting armholes and the bloomers were not shorter than four inches above the knee.

Men were required to have suits that had "a shirt effect or skirt worn outside of the trunks," and the trunks weren't allowed to be shorter than four inches above the knee.

All suits were to be made of nontransparent material, and those in wet "bathing costumes" couldn't loiter in the pavilion. Anyone indulging in profanity or indecent language could be taken into custody by attendants or officers without warning.

During the 1920s and '30s, smaller pavilions and improvements were added to the park, including a refreshment stand, a donation of ducks and a pair of swans.

Eddie's Grill

Time seems to slow down at Eddie's Grill. Outside, drivers buzz by in modern cars and people walk down the street with cellphones to their ears, but inside, it's 1950, the year the grill opened. "The juke box is at your table. The lemonade is icy cold and freshly squeezed. The root beer is straight out of the barrel. The hot dogs are famous and the real Slovenian sausage, cheeseburgers and fries are legendary," reads the diner's website.

Thousands visit the Geneva-on-the-Lake (GOTL) Ohio staple each summer. It's located a block away from Lake Erie on Lake Road East. They know it will look, feel and taste the same as it did when they first visited years before. "It's always consistent. No matter when you come. You got a good hot dog ten years ago, you come back and still get a good hot dog," explained Eddie Sezon, who has run the restaurant, along with his family, since it opened.

In fact, the footlong hot dog (which cost fifteen cents in 1950) is his favorite menu item.

"We have the same menu that we started with—believe me, it can't be more than ten items. You can't have everything, so you've got to pick," Eddie said. "When you get busy, you've got to take care of those orders, and food has to go out good so you can only have a limited amount."

Eddie would know, because even in his nineties, he still works at the restaurant each day, from 1:00 p.m. to close.

"Sometimes you see three generations, and they keep coming. They bring their grandson and introduce them to you," said Eddie.

Left: Eddie's Grill in Geneva-on-the-Lake, July 2022. *Courtesy of Rich Macklen.*

Below: Geneva-on-the-Lake bathing beach, 1949. *Author's collection.*

Opposite: The Casino Dance Hall in Geneva-on-the-Lake, 1930s/40s. *Author's collection.*

Eddie is as much a part of Geneva-on-the Lake as his iconic grill. When he was only twelve years old, he worked at the dance hall (that closed in the 1970s), and then for the next few years, he worked at the games across the street. He said the area was different back then. "I saw people walking on the sidewalk. Then there was a beach and lots of people walking with their kids carrying innertubes in the afternoon, but now there's no beach."

According to a 2013 *Ohio* magazine article by former Eddie's Grill short-order cook John Gladden, Eddie started his business when he was

seventeen years old in 1949, when he answered an advertisement in *Popular Mechanics* offering blueprints for a build-your-own Richardson Root Beer stand. "With support from his parents and a lot of sweat equity, a North Coast icon was born."

Eddie saved up money from his other jobs for five years, and with some additional financial help from his parents, he signed a three-year lease for the land, paying $300 a year for the corner lot. He bought the lot when the lease was up. However, instead of making it just like the root beer stand, he decided to make it a little different, with a flat roof and stools added along part of the perimeter.

Three years into business, the hot dog stand next to Eddie went up for sale, so he bought it and began expanding to add ice cream to his diner.

According to a 2016 interview with Eddie that Carl Feather conducted for the Summer Fun Heritage Trail, Eddie said he and his family decided, in 1959, to tear it all down and build the grill that stands today.

Eddie's Slovenian immigrant parents, Mary and Frank Sezon, who instilled a strong work ethic in Eddie and sister Rose Marie, also helped at the grill. According to Feather's interview, Eddie's mother had been in business in Europe years before, and her father had a bakery in Cleveland, so she was always a big help.

"My parents helped me. Everyone put everything they had into it," Eddie told Feather. Eddie's family pitched in even more for a few years while he was in college and then when he got drafted and stationed in Missouri and

Germany. "And my mother, sister, and dad ran it the best they could all while I was gone."

The restaurant has generally remained open throughout every summer since opening, except in 1965, when Eddie recalled the grill closed for several days during the riots that took place in GOTL.

According to a July 5, 1965 article in the *Cleveland Press*, the riot broke out on July 3, seemingly with a fight between two young men. "But for mysterious reasons known only to the participants, it became a four-hour brawl. Hundreds of young people participated. Windows were broken, cars battered and policemen injured. It was an ugly mess," the article reads. Two hundred officers were brought in, and several dozen "rebels without a cause" were arrested.

Today, Eddie is happy to say the grill is still a family affair, run by Eddie and his wife, Anne; his daughters, Jennifer (whom he says runs the place) and Marianne (a common pleas judge); and his grandchildren. Eddie said his grandson Graydon Brugger is studying at John Carrol University and hopes to one day take over managing the family business.

It's clear Eddie is so proud of his family and the business they have built and run together, starting from the ground up. The dream of an ambitious teen has lasted a lifetime. It's a business locals count on as part of their summertime tradition, and it is still being introduced to new visitors.

In a world where change is constant and people race to keep up, Eddie has found the right recipes (beginning with his mother's homemade Old World recipe for chili) to create a business that stays the same, one that people can count on to be exactly as it was when it first opened seventy-five years ago.

Anchor Bar

Late one evening in 1964, Dominic Bellissimo was bartending behind the counter at the Anchor Bar. It was a small restaurant located near the foot of Lake Erie at 1047 Main Street in Buffalo, New York. His parents opened the bar in 1935, and an iconic sign was hanging above the front door in their honor that originally read: "Frank and Teressa's Anchor Bar." The bar was named after its owners and was located close to the lake. Signs in the windows and on the side of the building advertised the bar's "famous Italian and American food."

While Dominic was working, a group of his friends arrived at the bar and said they were hungry, so he asked his mother, Teressa, if she could make

Anchor Bar in Buffalo, New York, 1935. *Courtesy of the Anchor Bar.*

something for them to eat. Little did she know that her son's simple request would inspire her to try something different and create what has become a Buffalo classic—making that restaurant as famous as the sign first read.

"They looked like chicken wings, a part of the chicken that usually went into the stock pot for soup," reads the restaurant's website. "Teressa had deep fried the wings and flavored them with a secret sauce. The wings were an instant hit, and it didn't take long for people to flock to the bar to experience this new taste sensation. From that evening on, Buffalo wings became a regular part of the menu at the Anchor Bar."

The Buffalo wing phenomenon spread across the country—and even the world—as restaurants attempted to re-create the Bellissimos' recipe. The Anchor Bar has become a franchise with more than a dozen locations, but none is as famous as the first, which has drawn visitors to the birthplace of the Buffalo chicken wing for nearly a century.

6

TRAGEDIES AND TRIUMPHS

ASHTABULA BRIDGE DISASTER

On the evening of December 29, 1876, a Lake Shore and Michigan Southern (LS&MS) Railway Train was traveling blindly through a snowstorm. The *Pacific Express* left New York the night before and was nearing an iron bridge crossing over the Ashtabula River (called Ashtabula Creek in articles from that time) in Ashtabula, Ohio. The train, consisting of eleven cars drawn by two engines, began crossing at a slow rate. The engines made their way across. Then, suddenly, the bridge gave way. The entire train, except for the first engine, whose couplings had broken, plummeted seventy-five feet into the ravine.

An 1877 *Harper's Weekly* article on the Legends of America website described the moments after the accident:

> *The banks are steep, and the furious snowstorm that had been raging for several hours rendered it difficult for those who hastened to the scene of the disaster to reach the wreck. To add to the horror of the situation, the cars took fire from the stoves, and many passengers who were not killed outright by the fall were burned to death.*

Mr. Burchell of Chicago survived the disaster, and his description of the scene was included in the article:

> *The first thing I heard was a cracking in the front part of the car, and then the same cracking in the rear. Then came another cracking in the front louder than the first, and then came a sickening oscillation and a sudden sinking, and I was thrown stunned from my seat. The train lay in the valley in the water, our car a little on its side, both ends broke in. The rest of the train lay in every direction, some on end, some on the side, crushed and broken. The snow in the valley was nearly to my waist, and I could only move with difficulty. The wreck was then on fire. The wind was blowing from the east and whirling blinding masses of snow over the terrible ruin. The crackling of the flames, the whistling wind, the screaming of the hurt made a pandemonium of that little valley, and the water of the freezing creek was red with blood or black with flying cinders.*

A relief train from Cleveland arrived with medical aid, supplies and blankets to help the injured and transport survivors.

(The Ashtabula County Medical Center was created after the accident because of the lack of medical care when residents needed it the most. According to ACMC Health, community members recognized that a calamity of that magnitude could happen again, so they started the first hospital in Ashtabula.)

More than 90 of the train's 159 passengers and crew were killed, making it one of the worst railroad disasters in American history. The most well-known passengers were leading gospel singer and songwriter Philip Paul Bliss, known for "It Is Well with My Soul," and his wife, Lucy. A Cleveland.com article by Brian Albrecht explained that Philip escaped through a railcar window but went back to desperately try to save his wife, who was pinned in the wreckage. He couldn't get her out, so he stayed with her and they died together.

According to the Cleveland.com article, there were other heroes in the disaster, including Charles B. Leek, the nation's first Black telegraph operator. He "stayed at his post in the nearby Ashtabula railroad depot for 50 hours without a break, sending out news of the disaster, appeals for aid, and handling inquiries from anxious families."

According to Legends of America, the bridge was built eleven years before the accident. Designed by Charles Collins (chief engineer for the LS&MS Railroad) and Amasa Stone (Cleveland industrialist and director of the LS&MS Railroad), it was the first Howe-type wrought-iron truss bridge. Although the bridge had been tested with the weight of six trains, Collins was said to be reluctant to go through with constructing the bridge because he felt it was too experimental. But the higher powers prevailed, and the bridge was built anyway.

According to Cleveland.com, instead of using wood braces, which were commonly used in Howe truss bridges, Stone insisted on constructing an all-iron structure that used resources from his brother's iron-fabricating firm, the Cleveland Rolling Mill Co. (of which he was a stockholder). During the manufacturing process, air bubbles may have gotten trapped inside the bridge's iron castings, which then became weakened in the extreme cold.

Multiple investigations determined several factors played a part in the bridge collapse, including stress on the bridge, the cold and snowy weather, faulty construction and a lack of a careful inspection by an engineer.

Collins, who was responsible for inspecting the bridge and ensuring its safety, was at the accident site, and according to Cleveland.com, he reportedly broke down and wept uncontrollably during his testimony with a special committee of the Ohio legislature.

According to an Ohio Historical Marker at the intersection of Lake Avenue and West Twenty-Seventh Street in Ashtabula, "the unidentified were buried in a mass grave at Chestnut Grove Cemetery that is marked by a tall granite monument listing the names of those who died." Collins was also later buried at the site.

The tragedy led to several railroad improvements, including a standardization of reliable bridge designs, safety regulations and annual state-mandated bridge inspections.

Devastating Mill Creek Flood

The rain was relentless. It battered Erie, Pennsylvania, and didn't give up until overflowing water in Mill Creek burst the Glenwood Dam. Dozens of residents died in this early August 1915 storm, and wreckage was said to be piled one hundred feet high, with the possibility that bodies were buried in the debris.

"The property loss, early estimated at $3,000,000 was not changed by Fire Chief McMahon after he had received reports from big manufacturing plants in the flood zone," according to an August 5, 1915 article in the *Kane Republic*. "He estimated that 300 houses and 50 store building [*sic*] were laid low by the waters of Mill Creek sent out of its banks by a cloudburst and

Flooding overturned an East Twenty-Sixth Street streetcar at Eighteenth and French Streets, August 3, 1915. *Courtesy of the Hagen History Center.*

the bursting of the Glenwood dam. The city's loss on damaged culverts, bridges and water supply plant will be heavy." The article reports "many freaks of the flood" included undamaged automobiles resting in treetops and a house tossed on a hillside with "a wall of the dining room missing and the table undisturbed." Streetcars were overturned, and broken planks of wood lay piled in the streets. "But the power of the water's on-rush with its mass of floating logs and debris ahead was perhaps best shown where heavy stone culverts many feet high were carried for a whole city block down the ravine."

Throngs of people had crowded the banks of the ravine throughout the day after the flood. According to the *Kane Republic* article, "These [crowds] extended from Twenty-Sixth Street near Second Street, where the flood started down to the bay, a mile below, where it spent its fury in Lake Erie."

Telegraph and telephone communications were down, and trains were detoured while a temporary bridge was built to replace the washed-out tracks and bridges. Twenty arrests were also made for looting and disorderly conduct in the area.

Fassett Street Bridge Collapses

There were concerns with the Fassett Street Bridge from the start. Completed in 1896, it spanned the Maumee River, connecting Walbridge and South Avenues with Toledo's east side.

Not only did locals not like the look of the long, spindly structure, but they also didn't trust that it was safe either, according to the *Toledo Blade*'s archive site, TheBladeVault.com. So, city leaders brought in a horse-drawn fire wagon and firefighters to give the bridge a speed test to show citizens they could reach the other side in about two minutes in an emergency.

The bridge, built on the narrowest span of the Maumee, took a beating in the brutal winters along Lake Erie, facing ice floes and wind. In fact, the center span was carried away by ice in 1906. It was repaired, but the bridge collapsed in 1935 due to high winds. Luckily, no one was crossing at the time, and the bridge was once again repaired but given a five-ton load limit. By 1945, engineers said the bridge should be closed, but it wasn't. The next year, the bridge was hit by a freighter and closed for several months, and in 1954, it was knocked out of line by yet another boat. It once again closed for repairs and then reopened.

The city had spent hundreds of thousands of dollars in repairs on the bridge, and many debated whether it should be torn down.

Then on April 5, 1957, a squall with eighty-mile-per-hour wind gusts broke all twelve mooring lines from the freighter *Champlain*, according to the *Telegraph-Forum*, and the ship floated downriver and struck the bridge, taking out all three spans.

A photo of the Maumee River, taken from Walbridge Park, 1900–10. *Library of Congress.*

The next day's edition of the *Dayton Daily News* reported the *Champlain*, a 620-foot, 8,700-ton Great Lakes freighter, was moored at the old Baltimore and Ohio railroad docks for the winter in the Maumee River.

Bridge tender Harold Humphrey saw the whole thing play out while sitting in the control cab when the ship struck. "Helpless as he watched the ship bear down on the bridge in the wind-whipped river, Mr. Humphrey, said he immediately threw the switch to close the draw gates to prevent cars using the bridge," reads the *Toledo Times*.

Some initial reports stated a car was on the span and was thrown into the Maumee, but that wasn't true and no one was injured during the collapse.

The *Toledo Times* goes on to say, "The swing span was also knocked loose and set swaying by the high winds. Unable to control the span because the impact knocked out the electrical power, Mr. Humphrey had to wait until the winds pushed the span back into place before leaping to safety."

This was the Fassett Street Bridge's final accident. It was never repaired.

Steamboat Surgery

It was called one of the greatest feats in the shipbuilding industry—a sidewheel steamer, built in 1896, was simply split in half to transform it into a longer ship.

It happened on January 9, 1904, when the SS *City of Buffalo* of the Cleveland, Buffalo & Transit Co. was cut across its middle width so it could be lengthened from 208 to 340 feet. "The job of pulling the boat apart was done without a hitch," explained a *Detroit Free Press* article the next day. "Every rivet had been severed, every wire pulled, every steam pipe pulled from its slip joint, and when the strain was applied the forward part of the boat moved at the rate of about an inch a minute."

The forward section of the 1,000-ton passenger steamer was, according to the *Detroit Free Press*, "pulled by the engine of the shear leg of the drydock plant and two powerful horsepower capstans" and moved forty-two feet in forty minutes to lengthen the ship. The article goes on to say that "a remarkable feature of the whole affair is that when the forward section was stopped it was in plum to a sixteenth of an inch with the after part, which will remain stationary. Between the two parts of the divided boat will be built the new section, which will cost $170,000 and take until the opening of navigation to complete." The steamer was also widened by two feet. These

City of Buffalo along the Cleveland docks, 1900–10. *Library of Congress.*

THE UPSON-WALTON COMPANY.
SHIP CHANDLERS.
RIGGING
SAIL LOFT.
CITY OF BUFFALO
DETROIT PUBLISHING CO.

"Kirby's Masterpiece in Steamboat Surgery," January 10, 1904. *From the* Detroit Free Press.

additions were made to increase the ship's capacity by 60 percent without decreasing its speed or increasing its cost of operations. When completed, the steamer would have an additional freight capacity of 850 tons and eighty additional staterooms.

According to the article, the work was completed under the direction of Frank E. Kirby, a maritime architect and designer of the ship, along with the Detroit Shipbuilding Company and the Orleans Street plant.

The *City of Buffalo* was ready to return to its route a few months later, departing the Detroit dock at 9:00 a.m. on May 8 and arriving in Cleveland by 3:30 p.m.

Shipwrecked Crew Saved

The floor of Lake Erie is covered with shipwrecks. Many occurred so quickly, without the modern technology and safety precautions that we have today, that they became watery graves for the crew and passengers on board. Yet there are also incredible stories of survival from Lake Erie—like that of the *S.K. Martin* steamship.

Dick Tefft, with the North East Historical Society, brought this story to this author's attention and shared an article from their archives about the sinking of the *S.K. Martin.*

In 1969, the one hundredth anniversary edition of the *North East Breeze* reported:

> *One of the most disastrous marine wrecks occurred Oct. 12, 1912, and was attended with a thrilling and heroic rescue of the entire crew of eleven men and one woman. It occurred near 12-Mile Creek, west of North East, and the survivors came ashore near the Catholic Cemetery Road. The steamer sprung a leak and went down when the boiler exploded.*

It was a miracle the entire crew didn't drown because, as the article continues, it was one of the worst storms "within the recollection of the oldest lake captains, the waves rolling mountain high and breaking against the rock-bound shore with a mighty roar and sending up a spray that went above the 90 foot embankment on the south shore between Erie and North East."

An article published in the *Buffalo Times* the day after the wreck reported the 164-foot *S.K. Martin* left Buffalo with a cargo of coal and was headed to Erie when it went down in a driving gale around 3:00 p.m. near Harbor Creek. The crew battled horrific conditions for several hours in their yawl while trying to make the mile-long trek to shore. "The lake was a fury of lashing waters and every instant threatened to swamp the frail craft which held the 11 lives of the Martin crew. They rigged a jury mast and set a ribbon

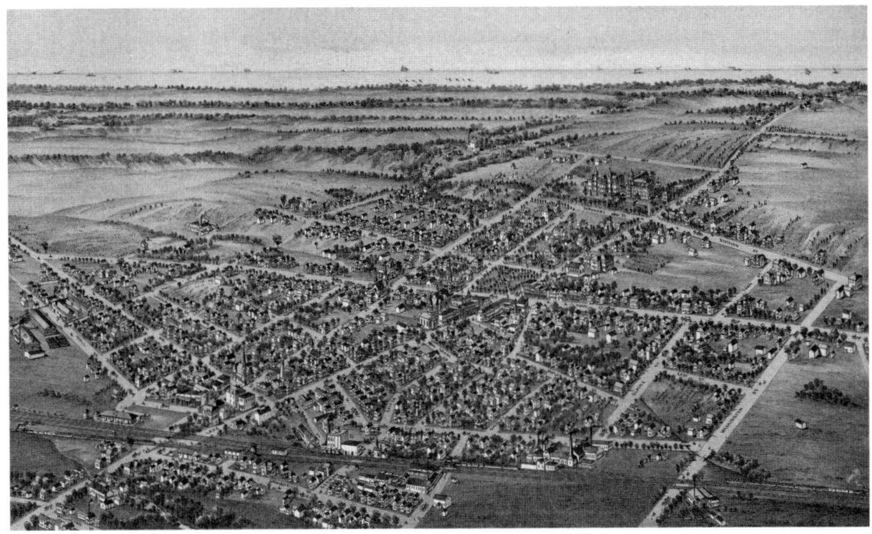

North East, 1896. *Library of Congress.*

of canvas to steady them, while the crew took turns and pulled manfully at the oars," reads the *Buffalo Times.*

The *North East Breeze* article credits captain W.J. Jack (spelled "Jock" in other newspaper accounts) with saving the crew, as he guided the eighteen-foot yawl stern end first through high breakers to a piece of low land that he first saw when his ship foundered two and a half miles away from shore. The article states, "The captain said it would have been impossible to come in bow forward; that he stood in the fierce storm sculling and steering while four of his men worked with might and main at the oars in order to reach shore."

Once the boat hit sand, several of the crew collapsed on the ground from exhaustion but recovered after resting. A reporter who heard about the shipwreck and the crew's incredible survival rode with them in a trolley car from North East to Erie, around 7:00 p.m. According to the article, the thankful group "spent the night about the city and crowds congregated about them as they told of their experiences of the afternoon." They were hardly wearing any clothes because they didn't have time to grab anything from their bunks on the ship. The captain gave them orders to put their life preservers on and climb into the yawl. However, they were given clothes when they arrived in Erie, and the captain gave each of them money to return to their homes or ship back out to Lake Erie.

The crowds gathering around the shipwreck survivors were fascinated. According to the *North Breeze* article "their stories of the battle with the waves, the blowing up of the boiler and finally the sinking of the ship were thrilling to the extreme."

Only six months earlier, the *Titanic* had sunk in the Atlantic. A fireman at the scene of the *S.K. Martin* wreck (named W.H. Manion, according to the October 13 article), with black soot still covering his face, compared himself and the other crewmen to the "gallant gentlemen" on the *Titanic* who'd earned so much praise. He said, "When it was found that we must abandon ship, we all stepped aside and Mrs. Bertha Knopf, the stewardess, was helped into the yawl and made as comfortable as the circumstances would permit."

Knopf was sleeping and suddenly woke when the ship sprang a leak. The fireman said, "She lost all her personal belongings, except a light dress she wore when she lay down after dinner. Mrs. Knopf did not attempt to run back to her cabin to get her diamonds, gold watch, also her clothing, but said: 'Boys, let us hope for the best,' as she crawled into the yawl. All the way to the shore she and the captain's young son were the bravest of the brave."

As for the captain, some said he had bad luck because this was his fifth shipwreck, but perhaps it was extremely good luck because he never lost a member of his crew.

Black Gold on Middle Bass Island

Middle Bass Island, on the western end of Lake Erie, has always been a quaint island. In the early 1900s, forty or so families who called it home were used to living life at a quiet and slow pace. So, when the murmurings of black gold started spreading across the island, it quickly built to an excited frenzy.

"Judging from present indicators, the islands of Lake Erie may have an oil boom that will rival that of Texas, and the residents of Middle Bass especially are no doubt already spending (in their minds) the fortunes which they expect will gush up from the ground upon which they live," reads a May 28, 1901 *Sandusky Daily Star* article.

According to the article, islanders arrived in "the city," presumably Sandusky, with exciting news of an oil gusher on the Henry Rehberg property on the island's southwest shore. It was drilled the previous fall "by eastern parties who obtained oil and gas leases upon a large part of the island, but it was never shot" (part of the process of drilling a well). The group chose the location because they were convinced there was oil producing rock under the islands. However, they stopped drilling when they reached a depth of 1,700 feet and struck Trenton rock. Then when the lake froze over, the crew transported their digging tools to the mainland by sled. The well was never shot, and islanders paid little attention to it.

That is until Henry, believing there was oil in the derrick on his property, decided to remove the plug, according to the article, "intending to take out a small quantity of oil to kill chicken lice in his hennery."

Soon after starting the pump, the oil in the well quickly rose to the surface. The *Sandusky Daily Star* article reads:

> *Yesterday, this well began to flow and immediately, following a lot of rumbling noise, the oil shot high above the derrick, 100 feet into the air. Reports are that it was a six-inch stream, and that before the well could be again plugged, many barrels of oil were carried out into the lake by the stiff northeaster that was blowing at the time. The oil flowed off on the surface of the water toward Rattlesnake Island for more than a mile.*

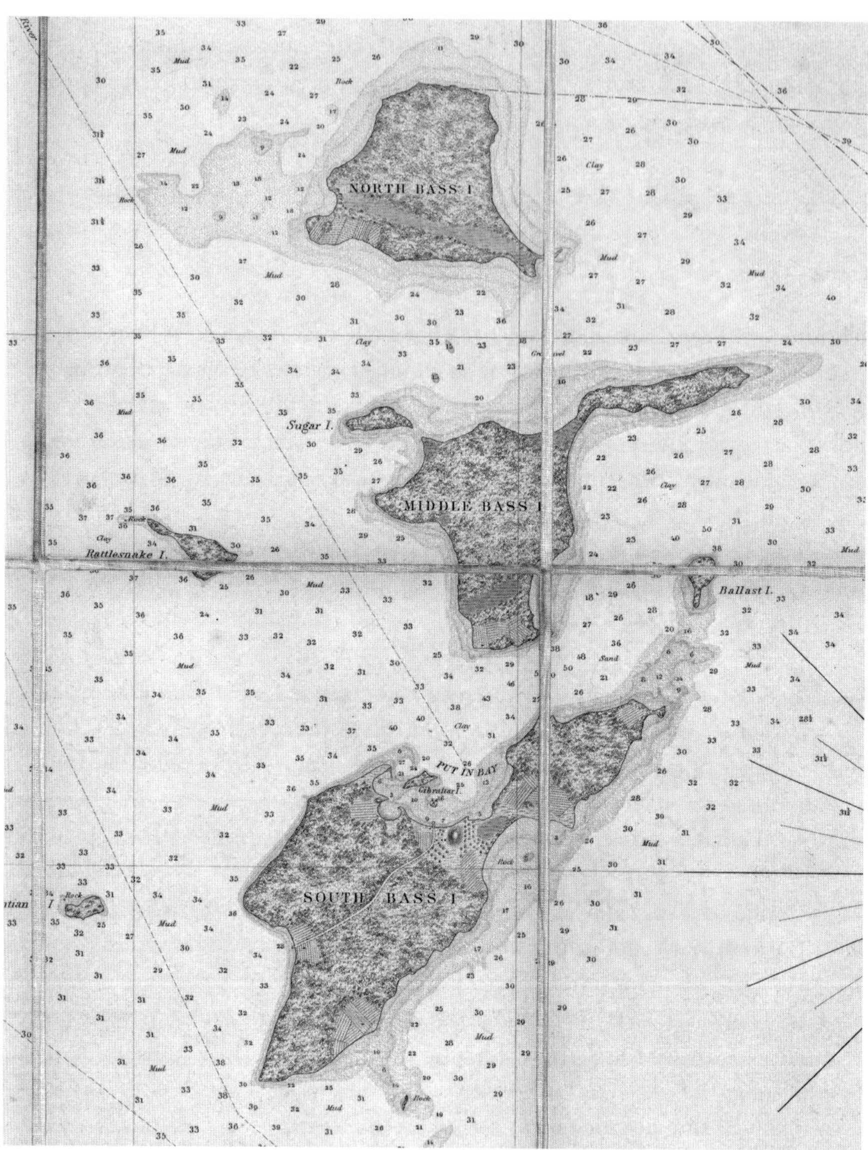

Map of the "bass" islands in western Lake Erie, 1849. *Library of Congress.*

Henry and those who were with him ran to a safe distance and watched as the oil flowed for about fifteen minutes before the well was plugged again. Some estimated that up to one hundred barrels of oil were lost in that short time.

"It is believed that in the light of yesterday's development, the eastern parties who drilled the well will return to Middle Bass and work that territory for all there is in it," reads the *Sandusky Daily Star* article.

The article says the steamer *Arrow* passed through the oil and had a dark stripe on its hull near the water line the following morning. Rehberg's nephew John was a member of the crew, and according to a May 29, 1901 *Sandusky Daily Star* article brought news to "the city" that the eastern operators of the derrick had been notified of the "spurt" and were making plans to come back to shoot that well and drill more wells.

Although islanders were still elated, the *Toledo Times*, quoted in the *Star* article, seemed to think they were overreacting:

> *The other day the well that was drilled on Middle Bass Island which was drilled last year by eastern people, and left with the casing in the hole, made the usual spurt that all wells make in which any showing of oil is found while drilling in the sand. They gather a "head" by a slow seepage, and sometimes the least disturbance will cause them to empty themselves. This was the case with the Middle Bass venture. But it was sufficient to cause the inhabitants 'round about to imagine that a Texas gusher had broke loose. The oil floated on the water and made greasy paddling for some of the pleasure boats. Strangers who had never seen crude oil afloat or in any other way became alarmed at the sight of it, expecting an explosion at every turn of the wheel. Some of them, it is said, began to make their peace with their God, and forgive their fellow men. The dear, sweet stuff had little knowledge of the rumpus it had so innocently kicked up.*

The coverage continued in the *Sandusky Daily Star* less than a week later and reported that islanders, who believed their community was sitting on a great fortune, were becoming divided, and "oils and anti-oils" were quarrelling.

Henry Rehberg was acting as leader on the "oil" side because the oil was first found on his property. "Against him is arrayed a small but fierce opposition, under the leadership of his nephew, Herman Rehberg," reads the *Cleveland Press* report. Herman owned thirty-eight acres on the northwest corner of the island, where three ex–Ohio governors had summer cottages and Grover Cleveland fished for bass. "These people on the island," said the leader of the opposition, "have gone crazy on the oil question. They are simply ruining the island as a summer resort. Let 'em kill themselves, if they want to, and fill up the island with their derricks, they'll never get any of my property, not much."

Rehberg's uncle Henry's response was that he should mind his own business and he would mind his.

A June 1, 1901 *Cleveland Press* article said fortune hunters were showing up on the island but quickly realizing there was nothing for them because R.W. Brown (known around the island as "Coal Oil Johnnie"), who originally dug the oil derrick, had a monopoly of the island, holding oil leases on about 750 acres. The remaining 100 acres couldn't be leased for oil.

The island was not only covered in farms and resort regions, but it was also home to wine producers. Herman Wehrle, the island postmaster, made half a million gallons of wine each year and leased part of his land to Brown, saying, "If Brown can find oil in my front yard, he is welcome to it. The more he finds, the better I'll like it. If he only discovers enough and I get my little barrel out of every eight, I can go to Paris and live like a king."

The oil discovery encouraged other investors to lease land on nearby North Bass Island. That's where Wm. Shires of Cleveland "took an option on 80 acres" after watching Brown's operation. He planned to keep a close eye on the situation, and if the oil "spouter" turned into a "gusher," he would start digging. "I think Brown has a good thing," Shires said in the *Cleveland Press* report. "I believe the island is full of oil and if he handles and finances the property well, he will come out on top."

The islanders were anticipating so much wealth that they believed their land had significantly increased in value. Henry believed his resort property was worth $5,000 an acre, while Wehrle offered to sell his farm for $50,000. (Just nineteen years earlier, when Rehberg began farming on the island, he plowed up cannonballs scattered across the island, perhaps left there after the Battle of Lake Erie, which took place in nearby waters.)

By early October, the *Sandusky Star-Journal* reported that a recently shot well was flowing at a steady rate of thirty-five barrels a day. "The flow of oil is considered remarkable, and those who have hoped for an oil boom are greatly elated."

However, just over a year later, in December 1902, the *Sandusky Star-Journal* reported the first well was averaging only about eight barrels of oil a day. The second well was far from being drilled, and those in charge of drilling had "met with bad luck." First, the walking beam broke, and then, when the well was drilled to a depth of two thousand feet, the rope broke and the drill and a good portion of the rope remained at the bottom of the well. Work was supposed to resume the following spring, but it's unclear whether it did.

The following April, Herman Wehrle, the local postmaster who hoped to get rich and move to Paris, was arrested for embezzling $5,000. According to a 1903 *Plain Dealer* article, "The money, it is said, was secured through the use of fraudulent money orders. Wehrle, who is about forty-five, belongs to one of the best known families on Lake Erie." Besides being postmaster, Wehrle owned a well-known pleasure resort, and his friends in Sandusky defended his innocence by saying his shortage was "due to careless book-keeping."

A few days later, according to the article, Wehrle was given $5,000 bond to ensure his appearance in court in June to face the embezzling charges. "Yesterday Wehrle was storm-bound at Point Pelee and the United States marshals were unable to reach him. His wife, in desperation, chartered a little steamer and in the teeth of a dangerous gale went to her husband, brought him back to Middle Bass and turned him over to the officers. She accompanied him to Toledo and is standing by him throughout the trouble. She has been placed in charge of the Middle Bass office in his stead."

On June 6, the *Plain Dealer* reported the federal grand jury returned an indictment against Wehrle on charges of embezzling more than $4,000 and issuing money orders without having previously received the money.

A few weeks later, the *Plain Dealer* reported the well at "Wehrle's place" was drying up and that only a barrel could be pumped per day. The hunt for oil would continue elsewhere, and the derrick and tools would be taken to Sandusky to dig a test well behind the Cleveland-Sandusky brewing plant. The oil boom in Ohio never did rival that of Texas, and it fizzled out as soon as investors realized no one was getting rich quick.

THE DAY NIAGARA FALLS WAS TURNED OFF

Unlike Lake Erie's ever-changing waters, the power of nearby Niagara Falls is constant. About seventy-six thousand gallons plummet over an eleven-story drop on the American side of the falls each second, according to the *Smithsonian* magazine. Lake Erie is one of the four Great Lakes that supplies fresh water to the Falls. "Once it travels over the Falls it travels from the Niagara River, 21.7 kilometers (13½ miles) to Lake Ontario. From there, it

The American Falls, 1905. *Library of Congress.*

makes its way down the St. Lawrence River and eventually to the Atlantic Ocean," reads the Niagara Falls website.

Since there is a 325-foot drop in elevation between Lake Erie and Lake Ontario, the eight locks of the Welland Canal can gradually transport ships up or down the lakes to bypass the falls.

The majestic roar of the falls draws tourists from all over each year, but for a short time, more than four decades ago, the falls ran dry.

"In 1969, the iconic Falls transformed from thundering cascades to a silent cliff face over the Niagara Gorge when the mighty waters stopped flowing for the first time in some 12,000 years," reads Niagara Falls USA. It began in 1965, when the local *Niagara Gazette* reported Niagara Falls was in danger due to erosion and rockfall that caused a pile of colossal boulders to tumble to its base. "Totaling 3.5 million cubic feet and scaling up to ten stories high, at some points along the gorge the rubble actually halved the height of the America Falls," says Niagara Falls USA. "Worried that the natural wonder could gradually deteriorate—and eventually become a series of rapids—the newspaper prompted a campaign for action."

The International Joint Commission was set up between the United States and Canada, and a master plan was created for one of the greatest feats of man vs. nature—shutting off the falls. For three days, beginning on June 9, 1969, the U.S. Army Corps of Engineers directed more than one thousand trucks to dump rocks on a water passage between Niagara Falls, New York, just opposite where DoubleTree by Hilton Hotel Niagara Falls sits today, and Goat Island. "Twenty-eight thousand tons of rock were off-loaded in total, creating a 600-foot-wide cofferdam upstream of the Falls," reads the site. "Once watertight, this dam diverted the flow of the Niagara River from American Falls towards the Horseshoe Falls. Once the cofferdam was finally drained, the American Falls fell to a historic trickle!"

The rest of the water was diverted to the Robert Moses generating plant's upriver intakes.

For five months, the American Falls remained dewatered, shutting back the normal water flow of about six thousand gallons a second to almost nothing, according to the Niagara Falls Public Library. During this time, United States and Canadian power companies and the U.S. Army Corps of

The American Falls, dewatered, 1969. *Courtesy of the Niagara Falls Public Library.*

Engineers were able to examine the site. Geologists studied the rocks, and workers sent down in safety cages by crane removed unstable debris. Aerial photos were taken of the riverbed's rock formation.

Although the beauty of the falls was gone during this period, curious tourists still flocked to the area, with 100,000 showing up in the first week to see the falls drained.

Although unstable boulders were removed and rockfall sensors were installed along the cliff face, many of the rocks were left in place to minimally interfere with nature.

On November 25, 1969, water could once again be seen rushing over the cliff, as the cofferdam was deactivated and the Niagara reclaimed its natural course.

7
Extraordinary Natural and Supernatural Phenomena

The Lake Erie Monster

She strikes when least expected, rippling up from placid waters near fishermen's boats or slithering her menacing, reptilian body across the lake's surface, causing nearby beachgoers to shriek and run for the safety of their cottages. She's been called many things—"Great Snake of Lake Erie," "Lake Erie's Monster" and "South Bay Bessie"—but she often goes by simply "Bessie" (which ironically rhymes with the nickname of Scotland's Loch Ness Monster, "Nessie").

She's been sighted on the lake for centuries and was even seen by the area's Indigenous people. Her first recorded sighting by a maritime settler came in 1793, when the captain of the sloop *Felicity* saw an over sixteen-foot-long snakelike creature. Then in 1817, a schooner crew reported seeing a thirty- to forty-foot-long, similarly shaped creature, according to the National Museum of the Great Lakes.

In 1896, a *Buffalo Courier* article reported that Captain Lina Beecher saw the creature at Crystal Beach, Ontario, and it was also seen "before excursion season opened" at Woodlawn Beach. "This came out yesterday, the people who saw the snake fearing to say anything about it sooner, as they did not want to be laughed at," reads the article. The article named several witnesses, including an architect, a leather merchant, the wife of the superintendent of the Connecting Terminal Elevator and a man who was working on a windmill.

THAT SARPINT AGAIN.

Reappearance of the Great Snake of Lake Erie.

PROVED BEYOND QUESTION.

The Monster Seen and Described By Reputable People Whose Names Are Herewith Given—This Time It Was at Cloverbank.

According to the article, the "snake" was first seen around 7:00 p.m., at Cloverbank, New York, where a row of summer cottages stretched across the shore, directly across the lake from Crystal Beach. The weather was pleasant, the water surface was calm and two men were headed out on a boat to set a gill net when people on shore began shouting to them about an object they saw in the water. The men began to row toward the object, about two hundred feet away, to get a closer look. One of them, the leather merchant Fred W. Sherman, who was described as a quiet, matter-of-fact sort of man, relayed what he saw to the paper:

> *It was a snake without a doubt, and if it was a water snake, it was the biggest one I ever saw. I am sorry now that we didn't approach it more carefully, instead of rowing toward it rapidly. We could not get very near to it, as it would dive every time. It dived three times, and it can travel like a streak of lighting under the water, for it came up in half a minute after every dive. It seemed to me as if it went 1,000 feet in 30 seconds.*
>
> *The snake's head was just about as broad as my hand. Its body was about as large as an ordinary man's arm below the elbow. A curious thing about it was that it seemed to travel with a spiral movement, like a screw. The people on shore saw four humps or loops on the snake, a foot or 18 inches apart. We could see five of these at least, though it was hard to count them, as the snake was moving all the time. Just before it dived the snake lifted its head out of the water, and then disappeared beneath the surface as quick as you could wink.*

A year later, the *Bryan Democrat* reported that "Lake Erie's monster" had been seen again near the dummy light at Pelee Island by William Crubb, the lightkeeper, and Adam Oper, the proprietor of some fishing boats. "While the latter was raising his nets he noticed the water was suddenly disturbed, and, heading his boat toward the thrashing waves, was horrified at seeing a fierce head suddenly upreared, while the thing's body continued to lash the water." Oper was said to drop his tiller and pick up his spear, but since the serpent didn't seem ready to attack, Oper quickly turned the boat to shore, where he shared his sighting with a crowd of people.

Opposite: Lake Erie Monster sighting, June 27, 1896. *From the* Buffalo Courier.

Above: Drawing of Lake Erie Monster. *By the author's oldest son.*

Both William and Adam agreed on the creature's description, saying it was about twenty feet long, with a broad head that was disproportionately large and a dorsal fin that extended along its back. "On either side of the head protruded horns like a catfish, and it had a formidable array of teeth. It seemed to the men that the nose was beneath the mouth. When it first reared itself from the water its underparts seemed white and fishlike, but as its rage increased the belly turned to a bright red." According to the *Bryan Democrat* article, its body was said to be covered with scales and when its head was above water it "kept up a loud, penetrating hiss."

Over the years, the sightings continued, along with news reports that made headlines across the country. In 1931, the *Times Union* in Brooklyn, New York, reported that a thirty-foot-long monster was spotted by at least ten people near Sandusky, Ohio. "H.E. Walsh, a fisherman, told of seeing the serpent while fishing from a small boat," reads the article. "He first thought the 'monster' was a row of small kegs in the water, but discovered his mistake when it raised a huge head resembling that of an alligator."

Campers near the mouth of the Portage River, near Port Clinton, also reported seeing the creature in the river. However, an *Akron Beacon Journal* article poked fun at the sighting:

> *This new discovery (made, oddly enough, during a dull period of news) is said to be absolutely different from anything else in the realm of fable. Nowhere in collections of folk lore will you find descriptions of a creature built like a row of kegs and supporting a head like an alligator's, Sandusky residents assert.*
>
> *Three different persons reported seeing this monster out of a bootlegger's nightmare. Dr. A.M. Houghtaling, city and county health director, winked knowingly when the keg part of the description came to attention, "The country around Sandusky doesn't seem to be very dry," he cryptically commented.*
>
> *Police Chief C.A. Weingates (get that name!) smiled expansively and said nothing. Meanwhile it is not of record that any Lake Erie excursion steamer voyages have been cancelled because of dry Americans fearing they will be splashed by any chain of kegs from Canada, with or without alligator heads.*

A few years later, in 1934, the *Windsor Star* reported that a man had caught the Lake Erie Monster—a 215-pound, seven-foot-long, sturgeon—and had it contained in a tank about twenty-five miles away from Windsor.

Reported sightings seemed to slow a bit for several decades, but they ramped up again in the 1980s and '90s. The *Dayton Daily News* reported the sighting of a "really long black alligator" in the lake. In the article, a biology professor suggested the creature could be a primate whale, like the Loch Ness Monster, or a sea snake that perhaps wandered into fresh water during salmon migration. Another biology professor thought the creature could be a very large sturgeon or a large fish native to the ocean that entered Lake Erie through Lake Ontario's Welland Canal. However, sturgeon usually stay near the lake's floor.

In 1990, the *Akron Beacon Journal* reported that John Schaffner, publisher of the Port Clinton–based *Outdoor Beacon*, a monthly tabloid featuring hunting and fishing news on and around Lake Erie, was receiving numerous sighting testimonials. "'The phone is ringing off the hook,' said Schaeffner, for 30-years a Lake Erie watcher and sportsman who is still riding the fence as far as an opinion on the monster's existence is concerned.'" John's office phone became the official monster sighting hotline, and he said he was leaning more toward the believers' side because the descriptions were all similar: "They all say it's 30 to 50 feet long, dark brown or black, about as thick as a bowling ball and with a wide tail." Many stories also said the monster had humps on its back and dove when approached.

Schaffner ran a contest to name the creature in 1986, when it was dubbed "South Bay Bessie" (partly due to the nearness of the Davis-Besse Nuclear Power Plant in Oak Harbor, Ohio).

Monster mania continued in 1993, when there was another sighting by perch fisherman Charles Douglas, who was boating ten miles off Vermilion during Fourth of July weekend. According to the *Telegraph-Forum*, the lakeside community decided to get on board with the excitement and encouraged businesses to "think monster." "The results include a restaurant offering a 'monstrous view' of the lake, a plumber able to handle 'minnow or monstrous size' problems and a car dealer's 'blowout monster sale.'"

In a 1993 *Plain Dealer* article, Huron's Charles E. Herdendorf, who was then Ohio State University's zoology professor emeritus, speculated that perhaps Bessie's ancestors were "trapped in waters that would become the Great Lakes during the last glacial retreat 11,000 years ago" and generations since then have survived and flourished on a supply of lake fish and plankton.

Not everyone fears the Lake Erie Monster—likely because there have never been any reports of injuries or deaths related to it—and some want a chance to catch it. In 1990, the mayor of Huron, Ohio, designated the town the National Live Capture and Control Center for the Lake Erie Monster, and Huron Lagoons Marina was prepared to house the beast in a 120-square-foot containment area that was capable of being flooded. The owner of the marina, Thomas Solberg, even offered a $5,000 reward for anyone who captured the monster alive. According to a 1990 report in the *LA Times*, he posted a sign at his marina calling it "the future home of the Lake Erie sea serpent."

So far, the Lake Erie Monster has evaded capture, yet it continues to stir the imagination of those of us who visit the waters of Lake Erie, always suspiciously watching a lone ripple or Lake Erie Monster–sized dark shadow on a calm surface. Perhaps it is more than it seems and something lurks below.

A Monstrous Beer

In the mid-2000s, Cleveland-based Great Lakes Brewing Company (GLBC) named a beer after the Lake Erie Monster and rebranded it with a slight tweak to the recipe and image in 2024: Return of the Lake Erie Monster Double IPA.

The Return of the Lake Erie Monster beer label. *Courtesy of the Great Lakes Brewing Company.*

The founders and co-owners of GLBC, brothers Pat and Dan Conway, started the brewery in 1988 after inspiration struck while visiting Europe. They wanted to bring fresh, full-flavored beers to their hometown of Cleveland and replicate Europe's fun communal settings by opening a brewpub-style restaurant. They hoped to distribute their beer throughout the region, so naming their brewery after the Great Lakes was fitting, according to GLBC brand development manager Michael Williams, who worked there as a server and tour guide before he went into marketing.

The company has also named beers after several prominent Great Lakes figures and events, including the fearless Battle of Lake Erie leader Commodore Oliver Hazard Perry, the *Edmund Fitzgerald* and Eliot Ness, the 1930s/early '40s Cleveland safety director who was known for bringing down gangster Al Capone for tax evasion. It turns out Ness is believed to have enjoyed a few pints at the more than 150-year-old tiger mahogany bar in the main taproom, which dates back to when the space operated as the Market Street Exchange.

The tunnel to the Great Lakes Brewery basement (exterior). *Courtesy of the Great Lakes Brewing Company.*

"Originally owned by Dan Rogers, the Market Street Exchange was a popular spot in the Ohio City neighborhood," said Veronica Bagley, the GLBC gift shop and tours manager. "Rogers operated that building until his retirement in 1901, at which point the building went through several owners until it shut down during Prohibition." At that time, the bar was cut in half and stored in the attic while the space was occupied by the Salvation Army. "After Prohibition, new owner Frank Krupansky took over the building and opened the Market Tavern, returning the original tiger mahogany bar to the space," explained Veronica. "Eliot Ness, for whom our Amber Lager is named, is famed for having enjoyed a number of pints at this bar," said Michael. "There are a few bullet holes in the walls of the main bar space that are rumored to have been shot at him!"

The story of the shooting was passed down by word of mouth from previous building tenants who ran a French restaurant and jazz club prior to GLBC taking over the space. "On the Haunted History tours, we dive into the story of Eliot Ness and his time in Cleveland, and his involvement in the infamous Torso Murder case, which, at the time, was the largest homicide investigation Cleveland had seen," Veronica said. "Quite a few people seem to think the bar has some 'spirits' (no pun intended) attached to it, and many staff members at GLBC have witnessed unexplained footsteps coming down the stairs, seen shadow figures, and have even seen glassware being knocked off the bar. No one knows for sure who the spirits are or why they're in the building—but definitely makes for some interesting stories."

Michael continued, "We do have thankfully written and direct testimonial that Ness would not have been shooting the bullets. That's because the Conway brothers' grandmother Margaret Conway was Ness's stenographer, so we have firsthand testimonial that he would not have carried his gun when off duty."

The structure has been a tavern for most of its history, and the building that houses the GBLC's production facility was once the distribution center for Leonard Schlather, a major late nineteenth-century Cleveland brewer. According to Michael, there are remnants of an underground tunnel that ran underneath Carrol Avenue to Schlather's brewery.

The building the tunnel led to was demolished in the 1920s, but in the 1990s, when Dave's Supermarket stood on the old building's site, tunnels were discovered in the basement during demo. "If you go into our building, a lot of electrical, storage, boilers and all that stuff is down there," explained Michael. "You walk down and turn right and there is our half of the tunnel, a little brick archway that goes into the side of the wall

Market Tavern and Herrman-McLean Co. on Market Avenue, 1960s. *Courtesy of the Great Lakes Brewing Company.*

and then there's just this brick wall. We've had the building since the '90s, so we may have known about that side, but the other side of the tunnel is probably in Dave's market basement."

Could the tunnels have been used to smuggle booze during Prohibition or secretly transport valuables? Maybe. But their real purpose is much more practical. "It was an easy way for staff to get from one facility to another when it was really cold out."

The three buildings the GLBC operates in have housed a variety of businesses, including a brothel, where the company offices now exist, and a feed and seed store that operated in the main taproom from the turn of the twentieth century to the 1970s. The feed and seed store was owned by a man named Herman Mclean, so the structure is currently called the Mclean building. "The Conway brothers are big on the authenticity of the building and neighborhood, and they left some elements there of the old Mclean building," explained Michael. "So, there's a scale that would have been used for weighing out grain so that's right behind the host stand, a fun little vestige from the past."

PRESQUE ISLE FLYING SAUCER

On a Sunday evening in the summer of 1966, a group of friends' day trip to Presque Isle, in Erie, Pennsylvania, turned into an evening of terror.

Eighteen-year-old Douglas Tibbetts drove his sixteen-year-old girlfriend, Betty Jean Klem, and her twenty-two-year-old friend, Anita Haisley, along with her two children from Jamestown, New York, to the peninsula. When they tried to leave the park that evening to head back home, Tibbetts's car got stuck in the sand on Beach 6.

The sun had set, and the beach was getting darker and darker as they waited for help.

"We saw a star move. It got brighter. It would move fast, then dim. You could see it come down. It was metallic, sort of silvery. It landed between two trees. It came straight down. The car vibrated," Klem explained in an *Erie Morning News* report, on August 1, 1966, the day after the incident.

After the police arrived, the women stayed in the car while Tibbetts got out and helped officers search for the craft, according to an August 3, 1966, report in the *Pittsburgh Press*. Tibbetts witnessed everything from the front seat of his car and shared those details with the officers who responded to their call for help. According to the report in the *Pittsburgh Press*, "Suddenly a 'formless' creature appeared from the bushes within five feet of the car, Miss

Beach No. 2 and Presque Isle Boardwalk, 1940s. *Author's collection.*

A sketch of the alien near the car on Presque Isle. *By the author's daughter.*

Klem said. She said it was six feet tall and had a head and shoulders but she saw no legs. She began blowing the car horn and the police, who rushed back, said they found her near shock." She was trembling violently and was almost incoherent. She told police she had heard something walking on the roof of the car and that "the flying craft 'sounded like the noise in a telephone receiver, only louder, of course.'" When she hit the horn, she said the creature ran off into the woods.

Police Chief Dan Dasconio, who interviewed Klem, said, "she appeared to be 'a pretty sensible young woman.'" He added, "I'm convinced these young people saw something."

The August 3 *Pittsburgh Press* article concludes by saying, "Only the day before, a Lawrence County man at the fairgrounds near New Castle reported he sighted a UFO and photographed it."

According to the *Erie History* blog, an article titled "Air Force Launches Probe of Erie UFO" ran in the *Erie Morning News* on August 2 and stated:

> *Officials would not comment on the investigation except to say that all findings can be released only by the Secretary of the Air Force. A test for radiation was made of the ground surface in the area of Beach 6 where the craft was said to have landed. But no sign of radiation was found by Erie County Civil Defense workers.*

The *Erie Daily Times* also reported that strange imprints were found in the sand in the morning hours following the incident, and one of the investigating officers took plaster casts of some of the tracks. Samples were taken of wet sand at the site that, unlike other substances, didn't evaporate quickly on the beach; it was described as odorless and sticky to the touch. An analysis by the air force determined it was a form of silicon.

Scratches and dents were also found on Tibbetts's car.

According to the *Erie History* blog, the headline in the *Erie Morning News* on August 5, declared, "Peninsula Ruled Safe After UFO Investigation," and by August 12, the paper's headline read, "Monster a Bear? Police Chief Says No."

Other UFO sightings were reported around the same time. For example, the *Pocono Record* reported two Erie newsmen saw two bright objects in the sky on August 3, 1966. The paper said it was the third day strange objects were seen in the skies over Lake Erie. "Dennis Buckel of radio station WJET said he saw and photographed what looked like a fast moving bright star. Jerry Trembley of WJET said he saw the same object about two hours later and another strange cluster of flashing lights," the article reads. This was only a few days after the Presque Isle sighting, and they are among many sightings that haven't officially been solved.

Sandusky: Ice Capital of the Great Lakes

Lake Erie turns into another world in the winter. Frigid wind whips off the water as it freezes into crystalline formations, sometimes looking like inner tubes of ice bobbing across the surface early in the season. The water then turns into thick, glass-like sheets of ice by mid-winter.

Sandusky Bay, at the mouth of the Sandusky River, is among the lake's earliest sections to freeze. Located on the lake's western end and averaging only about twelve feet of depth, Sandusky Bay has a long history of producing sought-after ice. According to Elizabeth Keefe's August 2023 article in the *Sandusky Register*, Sandusky ice was in great demand in the 1880s. It was in good supply, about twenty inches thick, and people relied on it to keep their food cold and fresh before electricity and refrigeration. "During this period, shipping hundreds of tons of ice brought great profit to the railroads that transported it, with big cities like Cincinnati and Columbus purchasing large quantities of Sandusky ice," the article reads.

"Pancake ice" on Lake Erie in January. *Photo by author.*

According to Touring Ohio, Sandusky was the largest ice producer west of New York City and became known as the "Ice Capital of the Great Lakes," thanks to its clear, crystal blue ice. "Icemen eagerly watched the waters of Lake Erie until they froze to a depth of 8"–16". For as long as *'good ice makin' weather'* held, Sanduskians endured 10-hour days of harsh winds and frigid temperatures for a daily wage of $2. The greater portion of the harvest was stored in some 50 sheds that dotted Lake Erie's shoreline."

An icy "wave" photographed on February 22, 2025, near Marblehead Lighthouse. *Photo by Gabe Leidy, www.gabeleidyphotography.com.*

A February 1901 *Sandusky Star-Journal* article reported that millions of tons of ice were gathered from Sandusky each season. In fact, Clevelanders depended on Sandusky for 90 percent of their ice supply. "This includes what is stored in houses and used for consumption, and later shipment as the demand calls for. Then there are hundreds of carloads shipped out of here every day while ice cutting is in progress. There is more money in immediate shipments than to keep the ice and retail it during the summer season."

There were three ice companies that operated twelve icehouses, with capacities ranging from ten thousand to thirty thousand tons. Fifteen thousand tons could be loaded into a house in just a few days, depending on weather conditions. According to the *Sandusky Star-Journal*, "There are elevators seventy-five feet long, reaching from the top of the tower to the channel below, and at every revolution the elevator lifts nearly six tons of ice to be deposited into the house. The cakes, as they are formed in the channel, and placed in the 'runs,' are forty-four inches long and twenty-two inches wide. Those that are loaded on cars are twenty-two inches square."

Sometimes, these channels extended for miles out into the fields of ice. Before the introduction of steam elevators, ice was pulled up the elevator by horsepower, with men stationed to grab the ice with pike poles to shove it down the runways and into the icehouses.

Hello There, Canada!

On a cool spring evening in 2024, I stared out at the wide expanse of Lake Erie. It was too early in the season for boats to be on the water, but as my eyes adjusted to the dark, I noticed a red flashing light out on the lake's horizon. Then another popped up—soon, I realized the horizon was dotted with dozens of red flashing lights that stretched across the visible length of the lake.

I called my husband, Brian, over, and we were both baffled by what we were seeing.

We started searching online for maps to see what was on the Canadian side of the lake, and I looked up the keywords "red flashing dots" on Lake Erie.

We discovered there were windmill farms, and a News 5 Cleveland article explained that a rare optical weather phenomenon was allowing us to see Canadian windmills and cell tower lights from the Ohio side of the lake. "The phenomenon is called super refraction," the story explained.

It's a bending of light rays downward toward the Earth's surface, caused by changes in the density of the air with height.

An impressive temperature inversion over Lake Erie caused the sunlight to bend downward enough so that distant objects not normally seen could now be seen with the naked eye. It means residents along the shore could get a rare glimpse of Canada from their own backyard.

The story, from 2017, goes on to say that the Ninth Coast Guard District said curious residents were calling with similar sightings back then, so they investigated and discovered the lights were from giant wind turbines in Canada.

This same weather condition, when warm air meets cold air hovering over cold water, is sometimes responsible for what appears to be "ghost ships" floating above the horizon on Lake Erie.

ECLIPSE OVER LAKE ERIE

When it comes to the skies above Lake Erie, 2024 was history-making.

Those of us who lived in the path of totality of the April 8 total solar eclipse knew it was coming. The hype was everywhere—even OREO made special eclipse cookies (which I bought for my three kids for the special day) with little pop rocks in them. The thin cardboard glasses needed to view the eclipse safely were stocked on countertops in libraries and convenient stores. People from all over were expected to flock to the path of totality, causing traffic jams and mayhem (although we didn't experience this in the eastern suburbs of Cleveland).

When the day finally came, the skies were threatening rain; clouds were thick the day before and gradually started to thin out the morning of the eclipse until the viewing became nearly perfect, with just a few white whisps left.

We were prepared. Our parents, who live nearby, were coming over for the big event, and I had bought all of the necessities for eclipse viewing: Sunkist orange pop (Yes, "pop"—it is the Midwest, you know?), Eclipse gum (for obvious reasons), Moon Pies, Sun Chips and even freeze-dried astronaut ice cream. The clock ticked slowly as we waited for the eclipse to begin. As it drew closer, we peeked through our eclipse glasses and saw the black

The sky over Lake Erie in Northeast Ohio during a solar eclipse's totality, April 8, 2024. *Photo by author.*

crescent edge of the moon creeping ever so slightly between Earth and the sun. It was starting!

The excitement was tangible, like a crackle in the air, amid the gravity of the approaching moment—something visible from our homes and neighborhoods only once in our lifetimes. The shadows began to grow longer. Birds started flying east, as if they were preparing to go to sleep for the night. I checked to see if our cat would notice, as there had been warnings of the confusing effects the change of light could have on pets, but he didn't seem fazed. It was, after all, around three in the afternoon, the hour of catnaps. When the long-awaited moment finally happened and the moon slipped directly in between the path of Earth and the sun, we stood in awe. There was a hush among us and a quiet among the birds and animals. There was a stillness and reverence for this rare and beautiful fleeting moment of totality we were all so thankful to share together.

I tried to capture it in my memory—the unusual darkness, even solar lights popped on; the deep blue, almost black of the muted sky above; and the bright yellow and orange glow hovering on the horizon. I tried to remember the expressions on my family members' faces—our mouths slightly parted in awe as our eyes were fixed on the sky.

And then, before we knew it, those few minutes of totality between about 3:13 and 3:16 were breaking . . . like waking from a dream, the world around us began filling with light once again. The long-awaited experience was over, but it will forever live in our memories. It's something I hope my kids will always remember—maybe it will inspire them to be life-long space enthusiasts, to pursue careers in science or technology. Or maybe they will only remember the feeling, the closeness of our family and the sense of awe we all felt as we stared up at the sky.

"The eclipse was really cool, but I wish it lasted for a little bit longer—like five minutes," my youngest son said. "It was cool because there was the Baily's beads and—I think it was called—the diamond ring around it. It was cool that it was dark and being able to look at the sun when we normally know not to."

The next total solar eclipse to pass through Northwest Ohio and over Lake Erie will come in 2099, but the next one to pass through Cleveland won't come until 2444!

Northern Lights over Lake Erie

Ribbons of light rippled across the evening sky. My husband, children and I stood on the edge of Lake Erie, mesmerized by the shifting colors and light that grew more vibrant as the sky darkened.

My oldest son described it as "bright and colorful," while my daughter recalled that it looked like "a rainbow and sherbet ice cream."

On this northern edge of Ohio, the northern lights danced for a few awe-inspiring nights, thanks to a major increase in solar activity. It was a rare treat, well south of the aurora borealis's typical vantage point.

"The northern lights were cool because of the wave in them," my youngest son told me. "It just looked like a swirl of watercolors where you swirl them all together some nights, and then some nights it's like streaks of colors."

We were soon joined by my dad and some neighbors as we watched one of nature's most spectacular shows unfold.

My coworker from my WTOL reporter days, chief meteorologist Chris Vickers, is passionate about weather and space weather. During this rare stretch of northern light activity, he regularly posted updates on social media

Aurora borealis and a full moon over Lake Erie, May 10, 2024, in Northeast Ohio. *Photo by author.*

to let viewers know when they would potentially be visible; he also shared details about their cause and some incredible images viewers sent to him.

"The northern lights were visible an astounding four times in the year of 2024. That is extremely unusual to almost unheard of," Vickers told me. He said this was because we are currently in Solar Cycle 25 of the sun's activity—an eleven-year cycle of sunspot activity that will last through 2030. He explained:

> *We have entered into the dramatic peak in activity during this cycle in 2025 that is expected to continue into 2026. This cycle is measured and classified by the number of sunspots observed. The increased solar activity can cause space weather events and geomagnetic storms that impact the earth in the form of the Northern Lights when a coronal mass ejection (CME) is detected from the sun. The charged geomagnetic particles interact with the earth's magnetic field and Ionosphere creating the display of northern lights.*

He said that in 2024, this caused a dazzling display of lights, reported to have been observed in all fifty states and Puerto Rico and even well into southern latitudes.

The first 2024 geomagnetic storm, classified as an Extreme G5 geomagnetic storm (considered the most intense level on the scale), occurred on May 11. It was one of the strongest in recent decades, and some research even indicates that it was among the top five geomagnetic storms of the past two hundred years. The northern lights were also visible on October 10 and October 11 due to a powerful geomagnetic storm that reached Severe G4 status. "This was a truly unusual and brilliant year to have the northern lights visible on multiple occasions and in such a brilliant way."

Glow to the Beach

Uranium Glass

The sky above Lake Erie is always worth a look, but as beach combers know, there is more than just sand to be found along the shore—if only you look down.

You can find beach glass on just about any section of Lake Erie beach, particularly near the sites of river mouths, glass manufacturers and even amusement parks. These pieces of worn glass are most often clear, light blue, brown and green, while vibrant red, cobalt blue, purple and pink are some of the most sought-after colors. Another rare kind of beach glass actually glows! It's called uranium glass, and it contains 2 to 25 percent of radioactive uranium, depending on the glass manufacturer.

"Uranium-infused glass was used for decorations, tableware, and cooking utensils," according to the Portage County Historical Society's website. "First created in the 1830s, radioactive glassware was produced mainly between the mid 1830s and mid 1930s, when WWII [World War II] tensions caused many countries to tighten production of items that contained radioactive materials. Interestingly, new uranium glass is still being produced today, although very few manufacturers are left."

Uranium glass was created by adding uranium to powdered glass before it was melted and shaped. The completed piece has a fluorescent, clear or opaque bright green tint.

Pieces of uranium glass can sometimes be found along the beach as broken pieces of dinnerware or other decorative items, and they will glow brightly under a black light. (Walking along the beach with a black light flashlight in the evening or after dark is the best way to search for pieces. You can also scan your beach glass collection with a black light to see if anything glows. My youngest son was excited to find a piece of uranium glass in his collection using this method.)

Uranium glass goes by other names, like Vaseline glass, which is a transparent yellow-green color similar to the that of petroleum jelly, and custard and jadeite glass (sometimes spelled "jadite"), which is opaque white or green-white.

Yooperlites

Glass isn't the only interesting object you may find glowing in the sand. "Fluorescent sodalite-bearing syenite" is a type of rock that actually glows orange under a black light. It can be found throughout the world but was nicknamed "Yooperlite" after it was discovered in 2017 in Michigan's Upper Peninsula along the shores of Lake Superior, where residents are affectionally referred to as "Yoopers."

The rocks were formed about a billion years ago when tectonic shifting caused huge volcanic eruptions, according to Michigan's 9&10 News. "One large body of magma in what's now Ontario, Canada, never quite made it to the surface," the site reads. "That magma cooled and became syenite granite with sodalite impurities in it." It was eventually scooped up by glaciers and pushed to the shores of the Great Lakes.

Justin Lynn is a rock hunter on the shores of Lake Erie and an administrator for the Facebook group "Lake Erie Fluorescent Mineral Hunters." According to the *Morning Journal*, he first learned of the glowing rocks while managing hotels in Michigan's Upper Peninsula. After moving to the Lake Erie region, he discovered them along the lake shore and "renamed" them "Neolites" in recognition of Northeast Ohio.

He says Neolites are most common on the eastern end of Lake Erie and generally look gray to the eye, but when a high-quality or 365-millimeter black light is shined on them, the light reflects from the sulfur ions in the rock and causes them to appear like they're glowing. "If you take that light out onto the beach and shine it, it looks like a campfire glowing," he said.

There are other reasons for glowing rocks in the sand, according to a 2022 YourErie.com article, including one that would likely create much more excitement than a Yooperlite: diamonds. "Most diamonds would fluoresce," Scott McKenzie, a geological expert and assistant professor at Mercyhurst University, explained in the article. "The closest [diamond] found near us was in Cleveland. Back in the 1960s, a little girl on a field trip found a greasy pebble. Her teacher thought it might be something, so they took it to an expert and it was determined to be a diamond. The little girl carried it with her everywhere until she lost it four days later, never to be found again."

8
Treasure

Does a slice of Lake Erie shoreline exist that isn't tied to a story of lost gold or treasure? Perhaps. But part of the ongoing lure of the lake is that it holds many tragic and fantastical stories, some true and some legend—or a mix of both.

The Legend of the Barrel of Gold

In Morpeth, Ontario, a story has been passed down by word of mouth for generations. Early in the French and Indian War, a boat left York (now Toronto), headed to Detroit with gold and supplies. When the ship was hit by a storm near Port Stanley, its crew threw packages and barrels of wine and liquor overboard to lighten its load, but one barrel of food was spared to last the crew until they reached Rondeau Point to restock.

"After being badly battered by the storm, the boat followed a course close to shore for the remainder of the journey," reads a 1939 *Windsor Star* article. "But when in the vicinity of Morpeth dock, so the legend goes, the crew spotted an American ship also hugging the shore, probably for the same reason."

Short on supplies and ammunition, the officer in charge of the British boat had the crew bluff their way past the ship, hiding their guns and pretending they were on a pleasure trip. "Fearful that the Americans might doubt their word, search the ship and find their gold, the officer ordered his men to place

A charcoal drawing of the lost barrel of gold. *By the author's youngest son.*

the money in a barrel, attach it to the buoy and throw it overboard. The ruse insofar as the British boat and crew were concerned, was a complete success," reads the article. "They were allowed to pass after a hurried inspection by the Americans."

The British crew returned with their boat that evening to search for the hidden barrel of gold. The article continues, "After a long search they found the buoy but apparently someone had blundered in attaching the buoy to the barrel, because the barrel and the gold were gone."

According to the article, researchers O.K. Watson, who was president of the Kent County Historical Society, and Dr. Fred Hamil, PhD, of Wayne University in Detroit deducted the legend was based on a real event—the loss of a military expedition that left Niagara in October 1763 to provide relief to Fort Detroit, which was being besieged by Native tribes. However, the expedition was wrecked along the shoreline of Lake Erie between Morpeth Dock and Rondeau Point. "The expedition was in charge of Major Wilkins and consisted of about 300 men, six cannons and a large store of ammunition and supplies, as well as a large quantity of gold."

While researching at the University of Michigan Library in Ann Arbor, Dr. Hamil found a letter sent from the crews who had wrecked on the shoreline and camped temporarily at the mouth of Patterson's Creek. The letter stated they wouldn't be able to make it to Fort Detroit to help because of their loss of boats and supplies and would be heading back. The letter was hidden in the butt of a Native's powder horn and carried to Detroit.

The letter began:

> *Dear Sir: IF the Indians who have the charge of this letter deliver it to you faithfully you will treat them accordingly. They are sent to let you know that the detachment cannot proceed, owing to the unfortunate delays by contrary winds and a more melancholy accident in a storm the 7th instant about 12 at night when we were put ashore here. Lt Davidson of the Royal*

Artillery; Dr. Williams of your corps; Lt. Peynter of the Platoons, with two sergeants and 63 men of different corps, perished near this beach. There are two boats with their crews missing. Eighteen Battoes and 52 barrels of provisions were lost.

The letter goes on to explain regret in not being able to accomplish their mission to reach Fort Detroit and is signed by "T. Moncrief."

According to Watson, "This expedition lost nearly their entire equipment which would include the paymaster's chest where the gold for payment of the troops and the buying of supplies would be kept, and doubt this is probably the lost treasure which has been remembered for so many years."

The gold, in 1939, was estimated to be worth around $100,000. If it does exist, it is likely on the bottom of Lake Erie, covered by sand and sediment, waiting for a strong storm and churning waves to push it closer to shore, where perhaps it will one day be discovered.

THE WHISKEY SHIP TREASURE

In the western basin of Lake Erie sits a tiny island, said to be at the center of a legendary tale.

As the story goes, on an icy winter day, just before the Civil War, a whiskey ship sank near West Sister Island.

The tale has made its rounds for years in nearby Monroe, Michigan, as a 1921 *Binghamton Press* article explains:

> *The mystery of the whiskey ship has been recaled* [sic] *more poignantly by a few of the old-time fishermen in these so-called Prohibition days.*
>
> *"Think of it—60-year-old whiskey! What a prize it would bring!" they say.*
>
> *Several fishermen have said they have an idea of the location of the vessel; that they have brought up bits of chain and pieces of wood that might have been a part of a ship. But they guard their "secret" in the hope that some day they may be able themselves to search the lake bottom and retrieve the precious liquid.*

Steamboat boiler inspector Wallace Tomey shared the story, told to him by old fishermen, with the paper. He said that when Monroe was a flourishing

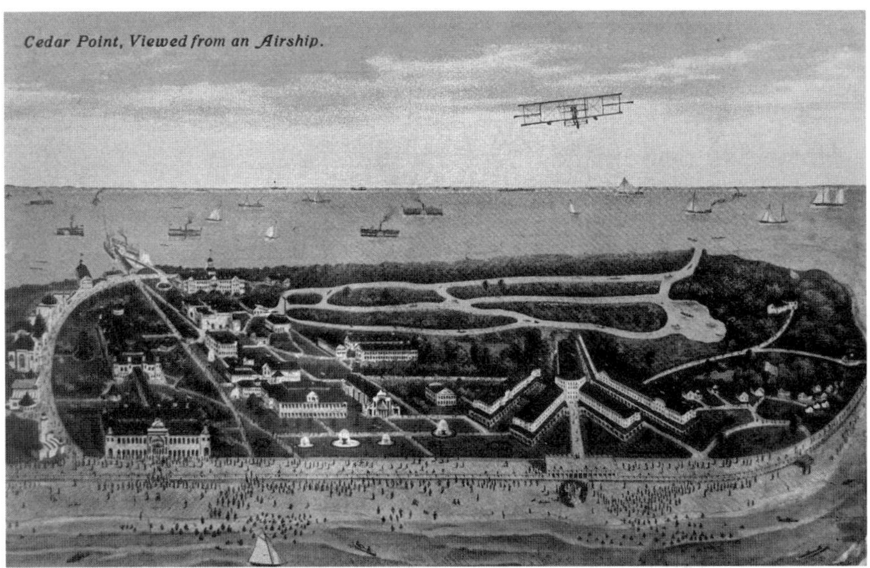

Cedar Point, as viewed from an airship, 1920s/30s. *Author's collection.*

lake port, a line of fast wooden packet steamers traveled regularly between Monroe and Buffalo. On one stormy trip, a steamer heading from Buffalo, with a cargo of stoves and whiskey, became imbedded in the ice a few miles offshore from Monroe.

The crew left the ship and its cargo and hoped to go back to retrieve it when the ice became firm enough.

"Fierce gales swept the lakes for some weeks thereafter and when a party set out to look for the ice-bound ship no trace of her could be found," reads the article. "It was believed in the shifting of the ice by the gales the vessel had been crushed and sunk with her cargo."

People searched nearby beaches in the spring, but no sign of the vessel could be found. However, according to the *Binghamton Press* article, years later, a cask of whiskey did turn up a good distance down the lake near Cedar Point, and it was taken to Chicago, where "the excellent whiskey was sold for 50 cents a glass."

It goes on to say, since the whiskey casks in the cargo were believed to be bound with wooden hoops, the barrels could have remained in the water for many more years without breaking up. "If the wreck could be located and only a few of the casks of whiskey salvaged it would bring a fabulous price and would justify almost any expense incurred."

$35,000 Rum Cargo Seizure

At the height of Prohibition, rum runners were rampant on Lake Erie, often working undercover as workers on "fishing boats" to transport booze between the United States and Canada.

In the early morning hours of June 7, 1929, one of the largest Lake Erie rum cargo seizures took place near Cleveland.

"A cargo of alleged Canadian whiskey and ale, valued at about $35,000 [equivalent to about $500,000 today] was seized by U.S. coastguardsmen here early today when they intercepted a tug, the *Neptune*," reads an article from the *Marion Star.*

The Coast Guard admitted the rumrunners would have likely landed their cargo safely had it not been for an accident. According to the *Marion Star* article, "Notified by telephone shortly after midnight that a fishing boat had capsized and two men were drowning, Capt. John Daly, of the coastguard service, put out with a small cutter and a crew to rescue them." However, as the Coast Guard cutter passed the East Ninth Street coal dock, the crew could see a red light flashing from shore, likely aimed at the *Neptune.* "Captain Daly immediately suspected that watchers on shore had mistaken the government craft for a rumrunning boat and were signaling it," reads the article.

Barrels of whiskey inside the rack warehouse at Hiram Walker & Sons, Walkerville, Ontario, 1900. *Library of Congress.*

So, the Coast Guard crew shut off their lights and cruised quietly, seeing that the *Neptune* was coming into view and seemed to be running just fine. "'Heave to!' Captain Daly shouted and a few minutes later the coastguardsmen boarded the tug," reported the *Marion Star*. "One man on the captured boat jumped overboard and it has not been learned whether he succeeded in swimming ashore." Another man, George D. White of Leamington, Ontario, was arrested. He confessed to having been hired the previous day in Leamington to run the tug's gasoline engine, and the man who had jumped overboard was the skipper, named West.

Navigation papers showed that the *Neptune* was said to be engaged in the fishing industry and was chartered at "Point Clinton, O" (likely Port Clinton). It was carrying a substantial cargo: five hundred cases of Walkerville, Ontario whiskey and two hundred cases of Canadian ale.

Lost Caves of Gold

On the eastern end of Lake Erie, British ships, said to be carrying gold, were attacked by the French near Dunkirk, New York. According to the blog *Lost Treasure in New York State*, some of the ships sank in the battle, two escaped and one acted as a decoy to throw off the French from capturing the other ship that was carrying gold. It stopped near the mouth of the Chautauqua Creek, near Barcelona, where the gold was said to be loaded into row boats, taken upstream and hidden in a cave.

The French later caught up with the sailors, captured them and tortured them until they revealed the location of the gold.

Although the French tried to find the cave, they never succeeded in finding the gold. "The cave is said to be visible on the east side of the creek during the winter," says to the blog. "People have tried to dig into this cave but have never found gold."

The second legend of lost gold was said to be mentioned in a 1921 article in the *Jamestown Journal*. Three French soldiers, carrying gold, were attacked by Natives while traveling the Portage Trail, so they hid in a cave about a half mile north of where Button's Inn stood. Because the cave was so small, they had to unsaddle their horses and set them free to be able to hide inside. They kept the bridles, saddles and saddle bags full of gold hidden in the cave. The soldiers left with plans to return to retrieve their gold, but when they came back, they couldn't remember which cave it was hidden in. It's

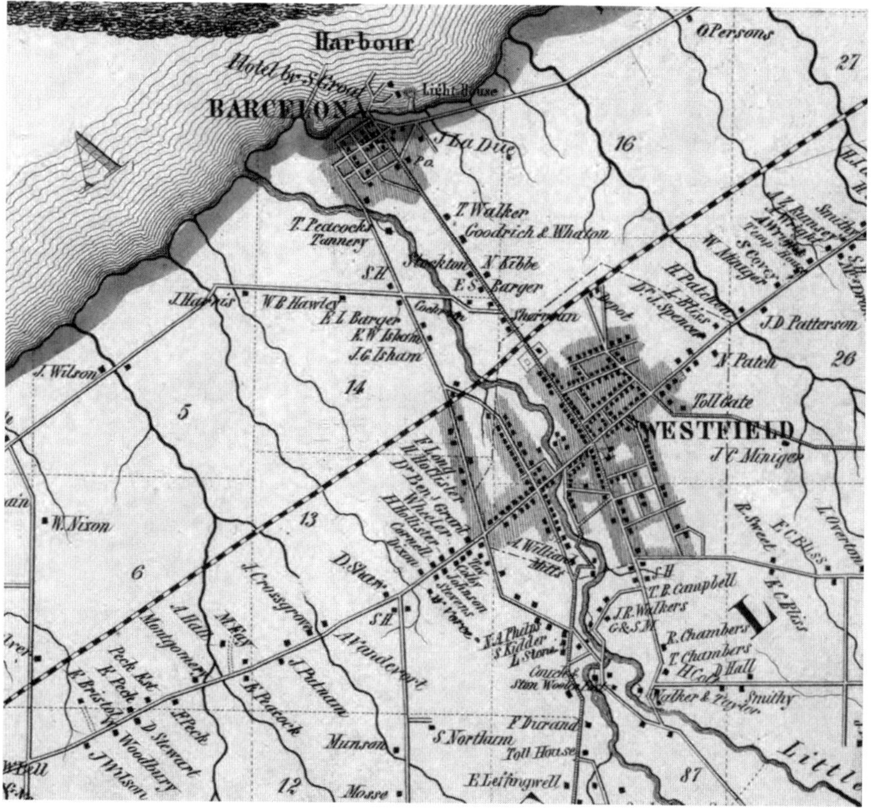

A map of Barcelona and Westfield, New York, 1854. *Library of Congress.*

unclear why the soldiers left the cave, but it has been speculated they had stolen the gold to begin with. Perhaps someone will find the lost caves and claim the gold, or maybe the stories will continue to be embellished over time, captivating the imaginations of children and adults alike.

TREASURES OF THE *G.P. GRIFFITH*

Mark Lasmanis wasn't expecting to find treasure while scuba diving in Lake Erie. Fish? Yes. Interesting geological features? Hopefully. But gold and silver coins? Not likely.

Yet in the shallowest of the Great Lakes, filled with shipwrecks, the possibility exists.

Mark grew up in a family that loved the water. His father, an avid boater, had a lakefront home, along with his grandparents, in Willowick, Ohio, and he spent most of his childhood summers snorkeling and exploring Lake Erie.

Years later, Mark and his wife, Annessa, purchased his grandparents' house and now enjoy access to the lake from their backyard, where his underwater exploring continues.

Mark was certified in scuba in 2023, but it wasn't until the following May, when he headed into the lake with a dive buddy for the first time that season, that he was truly surprised by what he found. "We went out so far and we came in and we started seeing these bolts, and nails, or spikes," Mark said. "And then to him on my tablet, underwater, almost like an Etch A Sketch, I wrote, 'Wreck??'"

Water conditions were calm and clear, and Mark could see the lake floor, at about eighteen feet deep, was covered with worn and rusted nails, rods and bolts. He immediately thought it looked like a debris field.

One of the first things he picked up was a large broken brass key. He started to wonder if it could be from the shipwreck he grew up hearing about—that of the *G.P. Griffith*. It was said to have happened in this location. His mind raced with possibilities. What could the key have locked? Something aboard the ship, like a door or a safe? Or an immigrant's trunk, protecting something of value they were bringing with them to America?

A broken brass key found in the *Griffith* debris field by Mark Lasmanis. *Photo by Mark Lasmanis.*

For years, locals who have heard about the *Griffith* have wondered what happened that night. Where did it happen? Who was on board? What were they carrying?

Many of those questions have remained unanswered, but we do know the *G.P. Griffith* was a six-hundred-ton steamship named after businessman Griffith P. Griffith, built in Maumee, Ohio, in 1847. In 1848, the *Buffalo Daily Courier* described the *Griffith* as being furnished in good taste throughout: "Her upper cabin is 152 feet in length, and 13 feet wide, and is embellished with views of American scenery. Her decorations are blue, gold and white. Her state rooms number some 56, several of which are double and furnished with French bedsteads."

While the *Griffith* was on its usual route, carrying passengers from Buffalo to Cleveland, tragedy struck in the early morning hours of June 17, 1850.

"The *Griffith* with her two tall stacks pouring fourth volumes of smoke, her paddle wheels thrashing through the star reflecting calm was soon several miles west of the Chagrin River," reads a 1981 newspaper article from the Willoughby Historical Society's archives. "All was tranquil and serene among the passengers and crew who were at rest. No alarm had been sounded. A passenger or two were aroused by the noise being made by the crew but thought the boat was nearing Cleveland and landing preparations were being made. Then someone shouted, 'The boat is on fire.'"

As the crew tried to steer toward land, the boat got stuck on a sandbar a half mile offshore of Willoughby (present-day Willowick), and passengers panicked. "The lifeboats were engulfed in flames. Capt. [Charles] Roby ordered the piles of boards, which law compelled all boats to carry for such emergencies, be thrown overboard. People were jumping over in crowds and there were dozens reaching for each board as it floated on the water. The water around the bows was now a mass of fighting, struggling humanity—crying, screaming and praying," the article continued. "The lake was so alive on all sides and thick with struggling people that others dared not jump into the frantic, drowning confusion. Immigrants threw over boxes and chests and attempted to float on them. Many were weighed down by the gold coins secured around their waists and in their petticoats and never had a chance."

Between 230 and 290 immigrants, including men, women and children, died. The sinking of the *Griffith* is among the top three worst shipwrecks on the Great Lakes.

As detailed in this author's book *Hidden History of Lake County, Ohio*, there were several theories about the cause of the fire: an oil applied to the ship's engine was flammable and explosive; paint, stored too close to the firebox,

The *G.P. Griffith* passing the Buffalo lighthouse, 1850. *Courtesy of Historical Collections of the Great Lakes, Bowling Green State University.*

overheated and burst into flames; water was removed from the tanks around the pipes days earlier; and the *Griffith*'s captain began racing another steamboat near Fairport Harbor.

According to a June 26, 1850 *Cleveland Herald* report, hundreds of immigrants were buried in unmarked mass graves on the shoreline and up on a bluff, near the wreck. This was done for several reasons: most of the immigrants had no local family, the work of recovering and carrying the bodies was strenuous and the weather was excessively hot. The ship's logbook was destroyed in the fire, so many of the names were never known.

"The wreck lies in about ten feet water, a hundred feet or more below where the boat first struck, and with the first rough weather must go to pieces," reads a June 20, 1850 *Cleveland Herald* report. "It is understood efforts will soon be made to raise the wreck. The smoke pipes are still standing."

A July 3, 1850 *Evening Post* article reported two scows were sent to raise the *Griffith*, but a treacherous squall capsized them, resulting in the death of crew member Wallace Ames of Fairport. However, nine men and a boy survived by clinging to the boat's rigging. Newspapers reported scows would go out again when the weather cleared to bring the *Griffith* to shore to salvage large mechanical parts, but then the reports stopped.

At some point, the hull of the ship is believed to have been dragged past the mouth of the Chagrin River, but this could just be hearsay. The Ohio

History Connection's Ohio Shipwreck Inventory lists the wreck debris as "scattered." According to *Erie Wrecks West* by Georgann and Michael Wachter, as of 2001, divers were able to explore the unburned hull, some machinery and portions of the wheel.

Although a plaque describing the tragedy stands near the wreck site at Willowick's Lakefront Lodge, many assume there is nothing of the ship left to be found.

For years, the only known artifact to be retrieved from the *Griffith* was the bell. It's on display at the National Museum of the Great Lakes in Toledo, donated by the family of the man who found it in the 1970s.

Mark Lasmanis considers himself an analytical and technical person, so he was skeptical at first that his finds were without a doubt tied to the *Griffith*. "In my mind I was like I'll give it a .0001 percent chance, but I know the rumor, so I'll entertain it. Little bit of smoke, so let's see if there's going to be a fire," explained Mark.

Above: Scuba diver Mark Lasmanis finding the first coin underwater in Lake Erie in the late spring of 2024. *Photo by Mark Lasmanis, www.greatlakesvista.com.*

Opposite page: Scuba diver Mark Lasmanis holding the first coin he found from the *Griffith* debris field. *Photo by Mark Lasmanis.*

Mark couldn't resist heading back the next day to see if there was more. He found the debris field relatively quickly and made a discovery even more stunning than the shiny key. "I started finding some other pieces of interesting cast-iron items," Mark said. "Then the shine of something caught my eye. As I focused on it, I recognized an imprinted crown and realized this was most likely an old coin based on the size and royal design, something truly special to find in Lake Erie. It made me think of lost pirate treasure I have seen in books and movies."

It was a thrilling and surreal moment.

Mark understood how quickly the lake could change and that if he left these finds in the sediment, they could be covered up and lost forever. So, before picking up the coin, he documented where he found it by swimming around it and recording it on video.

When he brought the coin to the surface, he could see it was an 1815 Brazilian silver coin. He started fanning away the sand at a random spot six or so feet away from where he found the first coin and found another, smaller coin that appeared to be a French ten centimes from 1807 to 1812. (It had heat and corrosive damage, and both coins predate the *Griffith*'s fire.)

Mark's wife, Annessa, is a teacher, and while grading papers, she realized she had a missed call from him. She texted asking if everything was OK, and Mark assured her that it was but that he had big news to share. "He insisted he needed to call me," Annessa recalled. "I finished my school day slightly earlier and rushed to my car."

After Annessa called Mark, he texted her a photo of the two coins he found while scuba diving, ironically in a stretch of water they had kayaked over many times without knowing what was hidden below. "We both were filled with excitement when he said that he believed these coins may be from the *G.P. Griffith* shipwreck from 1850," she said. "I was in utter disbelief! It is incredible that these coins and other artifacts that would follow were preserved in the lake just waiting for Mark to find it."

The coin may also shed light on where the passengers had come from. While most were previously believed to have been European immigrants, this find indicated that some may have come from Brazil. However, according to the U.S. Mint, during that time in America, both domestic and foreign coins were accepted as currency because the U.S. Mint, established in 1792, still wasn't making enough coins. So, it's possible the Brazilian coin was being carried as circulated legal tender.

Part of the *Griffith* legend over the years has included stories of coins washing up on shore, and an 1898 *Cleveland Plain Dealer* article reported large sums of money were, in fact, carried by passengers:

> *She had very little freight on her, but a good lot of money, and all of that coin. Most of the passengers, cabin as well as steerage, were emigrants, who had brought their savings with them to buy homes here. The money was almost all in French and German coins, and a good many people around here were richer after that wreck. Not unlawfully either. Nobody could tell to whom it should be sent, and their survivors had their own I guess. There was one man, a merchant, who after the fashion of those days, had been east to buy goods and was just coming home with them in a lot of big trunks. Well, he shoved all those trunks overboard, then jumped himself and came ashore, trunks and all, as safe as could be.*

However, the man lost a money belt in the water containing $2,100 (equivalent to about $80,000 today). As he was laying out the goods from his trunk on the shore to dry, the ship's second mate found the belt in the water and returned it to him.

The *Cleveland Plain Dealer* article reported that money washed ashore near the wreck for years.

> *One man, who lived right near the wreck, told me he got thousands of dollars—that he used to go in bathing, and feel it with his feet, and pull out two or three big foreign coins at once. Then he told another story about the storm that swept the wreck away. He said he was down by the bluff watching it, and as he looked at the great waves sweeping up, he could see gold and silver pieces all through them, and it set him nearly crazy to think he might miss all that money. It was death to go down on the beach, and he was in despair, when he suddenly thought of a scheme that seemed feasible and went rushing back to get a long pliant plank he had made the day before. Then he got a nail box, fastened it to the end of the plank, and started off on the most unique fishing excursion of his life, and a mighty successful one too—literally scooped up the money—and he swore that it was true.*

Mark's discoveries are significant because they are the only known artifacts from the immigrants on board. As he continued to dive to the debris field, the weather affected his search, exposing and covering different areas of the lake floor after every rough and calm cycle.

All the while, he wondered what he may uncover next. "Annessa and I theorized gold coins may exist and jokingly called it 'The Secret,' relating to the concept that the thought itself would influence the outcome and this potential discovery. I truly thought the odds were very slim."

But on a dive soon after, he saw the light of the filtered sun glinting off something round on the lake floor—he incredulously realized it was a gold coin. "It was liminal, with the intense yellow glow from the sun shining through the water," he explained. "This was my first time seeing this color and the unique yellow hue. Long gone was the familiar shiny reflective quality associated with gold, replaced with a flat luminant yellow from 174 years of being hidden in Lake Erie."

During that early June dive, he found several more coins. Some had visible high heat damage.

"When I saw the first coin, I had to make a mental check: 'Is this really real?' It was just extra shocking again to find actual golden coins that were kind of myth up to this point. When returning from the dive full of excitement, I sent Annessa a photo, with the newly discovered coins in my palm, titled 'The Secret.'"

Some of the coins' mint years were melted, but there was enough detail to search online and match the coins to designs that fell within the time narrative of the *Griffith*.

Like Mark, I also grew up near the wreck site in Willowick and rode my bike past, often wondering what really happened and if coins washed up on the beach. I was intrigued, knowing a shipwreck happened in my neighborhood, but it bothered me that so little was known about the immigrants who died and where they were buried. The details were sketchy, and I wanted to know more. I recently found an elementary school essay that I wrote saying I was going to write a story about the *Griffith*. Flash forward to 2021, and after extensive research, I included it in my first books *Hidden History of Lake County, Ohio* and *Lost Lake County, Ohio*.

Ironically, Mark first came across my books shortly after those first finds while researching the *Griffith* and Lake Erie shipwrecks at Barnes & Noble in Mentor. A short time later, he saw my books at Marino's Hair

Design on the corner of Lakeshore Boulevard and Lost Nation Road in Willoughby, where Maria Carlone, the salon's wonderful owner and my dear longtime family friend, generously sells them. Like Mark, I have been going to the salon for decades. Maria and the other amazing ladies at the salon know how passionate I am about local history and finding the truth about the *Griffith*, so they encouraged Mark to reach out to me. I'm glad they did, because on a June 2024 afternoon, when I was about to head to my oldest son's baseball game, I received a Facebook message from Mark, whom I had never met before, saying:

> *Hello, I may have some new information and possibly artifacts related to the* Griffith. *I am a local diver that lives in Willowick right on Lake Erie. I came across a debris field on May 21st and have been returning since. So far what I have found all seems to be in favor of it. If you are interested, I can share more details.*

I was stunned and immediately responded with: "Hi Mark, I am absolutely interested!"

A few minutes later, we talked on the phone, and although I was a bit skeptical of his claim at first, his description of where the debris field was located immediately increased my belief that he found the *Griffith* debris field. If I were to put an "X" on a map, based on my years of research cross-referencing historic maps and newspaper reports, it would be in the area he found it. When he started describing the fire-damaged items he found, I was even more convinced.

A few days later, I was excited to meet with Mark to see the items in person. It was incredible to think they could help tell the story of the immigrants who died that day, whose names and lives have been erased. Mark had the items laid out on a table outside. I asked if I could pick up the artifacts to take a closer look. I held the shiny key, which spanned the length of my hand, and a clump of melted silverware stood out immediately. It still resembled how it must have looked before the fire, with eight or nine spoons and some forks stacked on top of each other, possibly because they had been stored in a passenger's trunk. It was an overwhelming and emotional experience to hold it, tangible evidence of the high heat that ripped through the ship. I could imagine the terror those poor people must have felt.

I held a gold coin, damaged by heat, that likely last sat in an immigrant's pocket, money belt or purse. It was blasted with an intense inferno (gold's melting point is around 1,900 degrees Fahrenheit) before it plummeted from

Above: Eight to nine pieces of nineteenth-century silverware found melted together in the *Griffith* debris field. *Photo by Mark Lasmanis.*

Left: An 1847 British gold sovereign coin found in the *Griffith* debris field, scorched by high heat. *Photo by Mark Lasmanis.*

the ship into Lake Erie, perhaps, tragically, alongside the immigrant who carried it. As soon as the smoldering, liquifying metal hit the cool water of the lake, it solidified, preserving it as a sort of snapshot of that exact moment in time, and it has remained for nearly 175 years.

Mark explained:

> *People have an easier time making connections through physical items. Up to now, there were almost no tangible items from this event. The bell was recovered and can be seen by the public. That is great, but it does not tell the story of the people or the moments up to their final fate. Very little was known about the majority of the passengers. Unfortunately, a lot of information was unknown or lost due to record keeping limitations of the*

1800s. Over time, the line between fact and rumor became blurred. These artifacts provide new information to help fill in the gaps and have a better understanding of who and how these people lived up to the final moments of this tragedy.

I reached out to Alan Hitchcox, the vice president of the Willoughby Historical Society, who has generously helped me research for past books, and he provided access to the historical society's archives, which contain information on the *Griffith.* Mark invited Alan to view the artifacts he found.

Hitchcox commented after we met and viewed the artifacts together, "In my opinion, all of the items Mark recovered are consistent with what could've been on the *Griffith.* And the coins are the strongest evidence. Where else would they have come from, especially the gold coins? I view it like this: if a court trial were held and Mark produced the evidence he has, I'd find that he has proved beyond a reasonable doubt that he found the wreck of the *Griffith.*"

Hitchcox, who has taken a metallurgy course and worked for a metals magazine, provided insight into the makeup and melting point of the artifacts. "The melted silverware is also pretty convincing," he explained. "A wooden steamer and its volatile fuel would likely create a fire with temperatures far exceeding the melting temperature of silver."

From the spring of 2024 to that fall, Mark continued finding artifacts when diving at the site, including coins from France, the United Kingdom, Italy, Austria and the United States, and they all predate the sinking of the *Griffith.* He has also found metal clasps, tabs (with melted metals) and possible locking mechanisms (with melted silver residue melted into it) that look like they may have come from a trunk, several with molten metal dripped on them. This aligns with numerous accounts of trunks having been on the ship, including an 1849 advertisement in the *Sandusky Register* that states: "Lost. A black leather trunk with iron bands and brass knobs: the name of the owner, E.W. Sargent, on a brass plate on the front. The trunk is supposed to have been taken from the steamer *G.P. Griffith* on Tuesday night or Wednesday morning last."

Mark found other nineteenth-century items passengers may have worn or carried in trunks, including clothing buttons, a suspender or belt buckle, a woman's hair comb and "sad" irons. He's found large pieces of decorative iron that look like they could fit together as part of a stove. He has also found tools, including caulking irons, hammer heads and a chisel

Top: The faces of gold and silver coins with visible heat damage found in the *Griffith* debris field. *Photo by Mark Lasmanis.*

Bottom: The backs of gold and silver coins with visible heat damage. *Photo by Mark Lasmanis.*

Top: A decorative hinge and melted metals dripped on possible trunk tabs. *Photo by Mark Lasmanis.*

Bottom: A woman's hair comb, a buckle and buttons found in the *Griffith* debris field. *Photo by Mark Lasmanis.*

that he identified as possible shipwright tools during a visit to the National Museum of the Great Lakes in Toledo. They may have been packed with the intention of being used at a new job in the region the immigrants were traveling to. Mark has also found dozens of unidentifiable globs of melted metal. The types of items he has found, the high heat damage, the period they are from and where they were found all point to the extreme likelihood they are from the *Griffith*.

Above: Scuba diver Mark Lasmanis's retrieval of a Napoleon Bonaparte figurine. *Photo by Mark Lasmanis.*

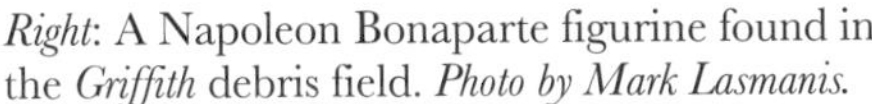

Right: A Napoleon Bonaparte figurine found in the *Griffith* debris field. *Photo by Mark Lasmanis.*

Mark said he thinks one of his most unique finds was a little brass Napoleon Bonaparte figurine. "Discovering a figurine of a person at the bottom of Lake Erie helps express the human element that was lost so long ago. This may have been a tobacco tamper or some other item from one of the French immigrants," he explained. "My ultimate find would be an artifact with the name or initials of a passenger, the crew or Griffith on it."

One of Annessa's favorite finds is the 1726 French coin with King Louis XV on its face. "The coin is nearly three hundred years old, which dates it as pre–French Revolution. This coin signifies that there were French people on board the *Griffith*, which was interesting to me," she said. "These coins exemplify the diversity of the immigrants on board trying to fulfill the American dream. This resonates with me, being that my parents immigrated to America in the 1970s."

Although Mark enjoys diving to the site, it isn't always easy or without inherent danger. "I once witnessed a boat getting very close to him and worried about his safety," Annessa explained. "I thought if at any moment he had come up, he would have been in grave danger. I watched for a good forty minutes before Mark surfaced, unaware of how close the boat had come." Another time, Mark's leg was injured while he was diving off a boat, and he had to wait several weeks before diving again.

Although Mark found dozens of artifacts in 2024, he plans to keep diving to the site and documenting his finds with photos and video. "I don't think there can be a definitive, end and there will always be potential for new discoveries. The debris field is so dynamic and dense with items. I can sift through one small zone of sand and find many items of interest."

During most of his dives, Mark has simply found items by swimming and using his hands to fan water and sediment away from possible artifacts. But he has also invested in a diver propulsion vehicle (DPV) and a scuba-rated metal detector. "This has dramatically opened the door for future discoveries by allowing me to cover more of the lake bottom and help sense what is below the rocks and sand."

Mark believes the historic pieces he has found are meant to be shared, so he has been working with the appropriate authorities, including the Ohio History Connection, to identify, donate and preserve his findings.

After meeting with Mark and myself in person and reviewing the items he retrieved from the *G.P. Griffith* debris field in May 2025, Linda Pansing, curator of archaeology at the Ohio History Connection, determined that all of the artifacts have historical value and placed them in OHC custody as property of the State of Ohio. According to Linda, these items will be stored and catalogued at the OHC facility in Columbus, in the *G.P. Griffith* Collection, with Mark Lasmanis listed as the collector.

"It's that next, real tangible piece to the story that was lost over time," he explained. "Instead of just being hearsay, here are the extra details of the immigrants carrying coins, the proof of the fire that was going on, the intensity of the fire. In the end, it's the last chance for it to speak on its own."

Mark wasn't expecting to find treasure, yet he did. However, the greatest treasure isn't the monetary value of the gold and silver coins but the priceless historic and personal value of these artifacts. They are like missing puzzle pieces to the past, fitting together to reveal a larger picture of the *Griffith* and the passengers who were on board that night. In a sense, the discovery gives the immigrants a voice to tell their stories through the artifacts Mark has found and those waiting to be discovered.

Epilogue

The next time you gather around a bonfire on a Lake Erie beach, I hope you share some of the stories you read in my book. But I also hope you share some tales that weren't included, because in doing so, you're helping to keep our region's maritime history alive. It's in the telling of stories that we connect with our past and with one another. We learn lessons from the tragedies, are inspired by the heroes and realize we aren't so different from those who came before us. If you live by or have ties to Lake Erie, you are a part of its story, woven through time and the people, places and events that truly make it a great lake.

A summer sunset over Lake Erie. *Photo by author.*

Bibliography

Akron Beacon Journal. "Hunt Serpent." July 18, 1931.

———. "Monster Witnesses Coming Out of the Closet." September 28, 1990.

Anchor Bar. "The Story of a Buffalo Classic." www.anchorbar.com/history.

Antell, Cheyenne. "Shining a Light on Uranium Glass." Portage County Historical Society. April 8, 2024. https://www.pchswi.org/post/shining-a-light-on-uranium-glass.

Applebee, Andrew. "Joe Root 'King of the Peninsula': Part 1." January 4, 2023. https://www.eriehistory.org/blog/joe-root-king-of-the-peninsula-part-1.

———. "Joe Root 'King of the Peninsula': Part 2." January 11, 2023. https://www.eriehistory.org/blog/joe-root-in-erie-part-2?fbclid=IwAR2LFVlW4Drfm9jlqShRM_fI222KWhp4JIbpXPL3IjvVqVQuP4lrMzAUe_o.

Ashtabula County Medical Center. https://www.acmchealth.org/about-us/history.

Austin, Dan. "*City of Detroit III.*" Historic Detroit. https://historicdetroit.org/buildings/city-of-detroit-iii.

Binghamton Press. "Cargo of Whiskey at Bottom of Lake Erie." December 24, 1921.

The Blade Vault. "Fassett Street Bridge Collapses, 1957." https://www.thebladevault.com/archive-prints-collection/fassett-street-bridge-collapses-1957.

Brady, Dan. "Mari-Dor Beach Cottages." *Brady's Bunch of Lorain County Nostalgia.* https://danielebrady.blogspot.com/2011/08/mari-dor-beach-cottages.html.

———. "Mari-Dor Beach Cottages Revisited." *Brady's Bunch of Lorain County Nostalgia.* https://danielebrady.blogspot.com/2015/08/mari-dor-beach-cottages-revisited.html.

Brooklyn Eagle. "Woman Diver Seeks Lake Erie Treasure." May 28, 1934.

Bryan Democrat. "Hissing Serpent." June 3, 1897.

Buffalo Courier. "The G.P. Griffith." May 4, 1896.

———. "That Sarpint Again." June 27, 1896.

Buffalo News. "Legend Based on Shipwreck on Lake Erie Comes Back Home from a Faraway Land." October 27, 1945.

Buffalo Times. "Martin's Crew Makes Valiant Fight Against Storm-Lashed Waters." October 13, 1912.

Camping with Sam Bananas. "Camping on a Deserted Island Next to a Deserted Lighthouse." YouTube. July 24, 2024. https://www.youtube.com/watch?v=xHUrvE6Tj6o.

Catawba Island Historical Society. "Likeness Found of Wine Maker Gideon Owen." April 25, 2023. https://catawbaislandhistoricalsociety.com/news-1/f/become-a-member-by-museum-opening-day-for-a-chance-to-win.

Catawba Island Township. "Historical Information." https://catawbaislandtownship.com/historical-information.

Cedar Point. "Cedar Point Timeline 1870–1969." January 7, 2021. https://www.cedarpoint.com/blog/media-center/cedar-point-timeline-1870-1969.

Cleveland Call and Post. "Finds Way to Raise Corpse in a Casket." August 23, 1958.

Cleveland Herald. "The Wreck and the Dead." June 26, 1850.

Cleveland Press. "Keep the Lid on Tight." July 5, 1965.

The Country Club. "About Us." https://www.thecountryclub.com/public.

Crair, Ben. "When Niagara Falls Ran Dry." *Smithsonian*, June 2019. https://www.smithsonianmag.com/travel/when-niagara-falls-ran-dry-180972198.

Dayton Daily News. "Lake Erie Monster? It May Be Sturgeon." June 17, 1985.

———. "Tornadic Winds." April 6, 1957.

Detroit Free Press. "Has More Rooms than the Cadillac." May 8, 1904.

———. "Kirby's Masterpiece in Steamboat Surgery." January 10, 1904.

Detroit Historical Society. "Archive Record." https://detroithistorical.pastperfectonline.com//archive/02D9A649-F1B4-4C53-9015-857202863739. (This link is no longer active.)

———. "The Gothic Room." https://detroithistorical.org/dossin-great-lakes-museum/exhibitions/signature-exhibitions/gothic-room.

Dunkirk Lighthouse. "Fresnel Lens History & Facts." https://www.dunkirklighthouse.com/fresnel__lens_history.htm.

———. "History of the Dunkirk Lighthouse." https://www.dunkirklighthouse.com/history.htm.

Eby, David L. "History of Monroe's Johnson Island." *Monroe News*, October 27, 2020. https://www.monroenews.com/story/lifestyle/nature-wildlife/2020/10/27/history-of-monroes-johnson-island/114507532.

Eddie's Grille. "A Summer Tradition for Generations." https://eddiesgrill.com.

Encyclopedia of Cleveland History. "Haskell, Coburn." Case Western Reserve University. https://case.edu/ech/articles/h/haskell-coburn.

———. "Morgan, Garrett A." Case Western Reserve University. https://case.edu/ech/articles/m/morgan-garrett.

———. "Polyone Corp." Case Western Reserve University. https://case.edu/ech/articles/p/polyone-corp.

———. "Wade, Jeptha Homer II." Case Western Reserve University. https://case.edu/ech/articles/w/wade-jeptha-homer-ii.

———. "Waterworks Tunnel Disasters." Case Western Reserve University. https://case.edu/ech/articles/w/waterworks-tunnel-disasters.

Erie History. "UFO Sightings at Presque Isle State Park." January 3, 2023. https://eriehistory.blogspot.com/2023/01/ufo-sightings-at-presque-isle-state-park.html.

Erie Morning News. August 1, 1966.

Feather, Carl. *Ashtabula Harbor, Ohio: A History of the World's Greatest Iron Ore Receiving Port.* The Feather Cottage Media, 2017.

———. "Eddie's Grill at Geneva-on-the-Lake, Ashtabula, Ohio." Wandering Back-Roads W.Va. YouTube. March 12, 2015. https://www.youtube.com/watch?v=0fkoJ4z2e-Q.

Fraser, Chad. *Lake Erie Stories: Struggle and Survival on a Freshwater Ocean.* Dundurn Press, 2008.

Genoa Gazette. "Cedar Point Season Opens." June 27, 1924.

Gideon Owen. "Our Roots." https://www.gideonowenwine.com/our-roots.

Gladden, John. "My Ohio: Lessons in Short Order." *Ohio*, July 2013. https://www.ohiomagazine.com/ohio-life/article/my-ohio-lessons-in-short-order.

Glaser, Susan. "Marblehead Lighthouse Celebrates 200 Years, a Beacon for Ohio and the Great Lakes." Cleveland.com. May 18, 2023. https://www.cleveland.com/travel/2022/05/marblehead-lighthouse-celebrates-200-years-a-beacon-for-ohio-and-the-great-lakes.html.

Gora, Michael. *The History of Middle Island, Ontario.* Lulu Press Inc., 2024.

Greater Cleveland Sports Hall of Fame. "Joe Mitchell." https://www.clevelandsportshall.com/mitchell-joe.

Green Book Cleveland. "Wakeman Country Club." https://greenbookcleveland.org/locations/wakeman-country-club.

Harper's Weekly. "Ashtabula Disaster." January 20, 1877.

Harrington, Kaysie M. "Southing Breezes & Gentle Waves." *Echoes*, July and August 2023.

Historical Marker Database. "Ashtabula Train Disaster." https://www.hmdb.org/m.asp?m=121524.

———. "First Cedar Point Road." https://www.hmdb.org/m.asp?m=41807.

———. "Lakeshore Park Main Pavilion." https://www.hmdb.org/Photos4/439/Photo439706o.jpg?811201822500PM.

———. "Monroe Piers: Southwest Michigan's Resort." https://www.hmdb.org/m.asp?m=201015.

Historic Detroit. "*City of Cleveland III.*" https://historicdetroit.org/buildings/city-of-cleveland-iii.

Hlavaty, Kaylyn, and Mark Johnson. "Rare Phenomenon! Photos Show Canadian Shore from NE Ohio." News5Cleveland. April 19, 2017. https://www.news5cleveland.com/weather/weather-news/have-you-seen-red-lights-on-lake-erie-theres-an-explanation-for-the-rare-weather-phenomenon.

The Journal (Lorain, OH). "Last Runs of the J.F. Reagan." December 16, 1979.

Kane Republic. "Erie Dead Toll Is Now 27; More Bodies Are in the Debris." August 5, 1915.

Kennard, Jim. "Great Lakes Treasure Ship Found." Shipwreck World. June 2, 2001. https://www.shipwreckworld.com/articles/great-lakes-treasure-ship-found.

Lake Shore Visitor. "Fr. Dugan Host at May Walk." May 16, 1930.

———. "Houseboats Are a World of Fun." June 24, 1960.

———. "Junior Choir Has Nut Chase." November 22, 1929.

L.A. Times. "Legend of Lake Erie Monster Rises Again." September 30, 1990.

Legends of America. "Ashtabula Train Wreck- Historic Accounts." https://www.legendsofamerica.com/rr-ashtabula.

Legends of Lost Treasure in Chautauqua County, New York. "Lost Treasure in New York State." https://wizzley.com/legends-of-lost-treasure-in-chautauqua-county-new-york.

Lighthouse Friends. "Turtle Island Lighthouse." https://www.lighthousefriends.com/light.asp?ID=271.

Marion Star. "Rum Cargo Valued at $35,000 Seized." June 7, 1929.

Mediak, Gabrielle. "Exploring Dunkirk's Historic Said to Be Haunted Lighthouse." WIVB. October 25, 2021. https://www.wivb.com/news/local-news/western-new-york/chautauqua-county/dunkirk/exploring-dunkirks-historic-said-to-be-haunted-lighthouse.

Middle Bass Island. "Middle Bass Oil Boom Articles from 1901 *Sandusky Daily Star.*" http://www.middlebass2.org/1901OilBoom.shtml.

Midwest Guest. "First Cedar Point Road, a History of the Cedar Point Chaussee." August 14, 2014. https://www.midwestguest.com/2014/08/first-cedar-point-road-a-history-of-the-cedar-point-chaussee.html.

Miller Ferries. "The History of Miller Boat Line: Put-in-Bay, Ohio." Miller Ferries. https://millerferry.com/about-us/history/#1555770179113-bd7a495b-03b3.

Mitchell, Craig. "The Untold Story of a Lake Erie Nature Preserve That Used to Be a Fishing Lodge and Casino for Gangsters." Outdoor Canada. February 2, 2023. https://www.outdoorcanada.ca/gangstergetaway/?fbclid=IwAR30SrpQTiHrLGk2gahZ9z26TkrZGNLIPhi0fJl_u2UzjuLv7SNRQw4wq3E.

Monroe, Lea. "The Haunted Lighthouse in Dunkirk that Will Send Shivers Up Your Spine." Only in Your State. https://www.onlyinyourstate.com/experiences/new-york/haunted-lighthouse-buffalo.

Monroe, Michigan. "River Raisin Legacy Project." https://www.monroemi.gov/c_i_t_y_h_a_l_l/departments/water__wastewater/river_raisin_legacy_project.

Morning Journal. "Sailors Get Food for Body, Heart in Lorain." June 27, 1940.

Morris, Corey. "Are There Glowing Rocks in Erie?" YourErie.com. https://www.yourerie.com/news/local-news/are-there-glowing-rocks-in-erie.

Murphy, Kara. "Enjoying the Ride." *Lake Erie Living,* July/August 2021. https://lakeerieliving.com/articles/2021-julyaugust/enjoying-the-ride.

National Park Service. "Remember the Raisin." https://www.nps.gov/rira/index.htm.

Naval History and Heritage Command. "The Evolution of Ship Naming in the U.S. Navy." June 5, 2024. https://www.history.navy.mil/browse-by-topic/heritage/customs-and-traditions0/ship-naming/the-evolution-of-ship-naming-in-the-u-s--navy.html.

Nelson, S.B. *Nelson's Biographical Dictionary and Historical Reference Book of Erie County.* S.B. Nelson, 1896.

Niagara Falls Tourism. "Where Does the Water Come From." https://www.niagarafallstourism.com/blog/where-does-the-water-come-from. (This link is no longer active.)
Niagara Falls USA. "When and Why the Falls Stopped Flowing." https://www.niagarafallsusa.com/the-source/when-and-why-the-falls-stopped-flowing. (This link is no longer active.)
9 and 10 News. "Yooperlites: Michigan's 'Newest' Rock (That's One Billion Years Old)." July 7, 2023. https://www.9and10news.com/2023/07/07/yooperlites-michigans-newest-rock-thats-one-billion-years-old/#:~:text=Where%20do%20they%20come%20from,it%20might%20split%20in%20two.
North East Breeze. "Steamer Martin, Coal Laden and Leaking Blows Up Off Twelve-Mile Creek; Heroic Rescue Saves the Crew." 1969.
O'Connell, Wil, and Pat O'Connell. *Ohio Lighthouses.* Images of America. Arcadia Publishing, 2011.
Pittsburgh Press. "Prober Keeps Mum on Erie UFO Report." August 3, 1966.
Plain Dealer. "Charge Against Postmaster." April 24, 1903.
———. "1920s Lake-View House Comes Complete with a Speakeasy." October 20, 2001.
———. "Postmaster Has Brave Wife." April 26, 1903.
———. "Postmaster Wehrle Indicted." June 6, 1903.
———. "Promising Well Relapses." June 29, 1903.
———. "They Captured the Lake Erie Monster?" June 20, 1993.
———. "Turtle Island Light Discontinued." April 27, 1904.
———. "The Wreck of the Griffith." August 14, 1896.
Pocono Record. "More UFO's Sighted Over Lake Erie." August 4, 1966.
Port Clinton Herald and Republican. "Deny Reports That Winery Was Closed." March 1, 1940.
———. "Jury Weighs Mon Ami Case in Federal Court." October 4, 1940.
———. "Von Baden Is Sentenced." January 31, 1941.
———. "Wine Company Officers Held on New Charges." January 17, 1941.
Randall, Mike. "Dunkirk Lighthouse Offering History and Haunts." WKBW. October 7, 2020. https://www.wkbw.com/news/local-news/dunkirk-lighthouse-offering-history-and-haunts. (The link is no longer active.)
Rhodes, Don. *Legends of Catawba.* Don Rhodes, 2008.
River Raisin Battlefield. "Battle of Frenchtown." http://www.riverraisinbattlefield.org/the_battles.htm.
Rochester Journal. "Gangster Suspect Taken by G-Men." January 27, 1937.
Sandusky Daily Star. "Island Oil Boom." May 28, 1901.
———. "Oils and Anti-Oils." June 1, 1901.
———. "That Big Oil Well." May 29, 1901.
———. "Wonderful Island of Middle Bass." June 6, 1901.
Sandusky Register. "Englert Nabs Speeder on Cedar Point Road." August 7, 1919.
———. "Lost. A Black Leather Trunk." August 14, 1849.
———. "Tale of the Firelands." August 20, 2023.

———. "Will Run to Cedar Pt. and Sandusky." June 27, 1911.
Sandusky Star-Journal. "Flowing. At the Rate of Thirty-Five Barrels a Day." October 4, 1901.
———. "The Ice Harvest." February 18, 1901.
———. "Prevent Progression in Drilling Oil Wells." December 11, 1902.
Silverthorn, Ann. "7 Things to Know About Joe Root, 'The Hermit of Presque Isle.'" April 15, 2019. https://annsilverthorn.com/index.php/5597/7-things-to-know-about-joe-root-the-hermit-of-presque-isle.
Soprano, Paul. "The Early Days of Commercial Aviation in Cleveland I: Before CLE and Aeromarine Airways." AviationCLE.com. July 1, 2023. https://www.aviationcle.com/post/the-early-days-of-commercial-aviation-in-cleveland-before-cle-aeromarine-airways.
Star-Phoenix. "Grandmother Is Anxious to Get Sunken Treasure." May 5, 1938.
Sun. "Hold Banquet in East Side Sewer!" Circa 1950.
Telegraph-Forum. "Fassett Street Bridge Collapse, Toledo, April 5, 1957." April 1, 2024.
———. "Lake Erie Monster. Real Thing or Just a Floating Log?" November 1, 1993.
Times Union. "Big Sea Serpent Seen in Lake Erie." July 17, 1931.
Toledo Times. "Ship Topples Bridge in Storm." April 6, 1957.
Touring Ohio. "Sandusky." http://touringohio.com/northwest/erie/sandusky/sandusky.html.
Transportation History. "A Pioneering Airline Launches Regular Flights Between Detroit and Cleveland." July 14, 2020. https://transportationhistory.org/2020/07/14/a-pioneering-airline-launches-regular-flights-between-detroit-and-cleveland.
Trusty, Sheri. "Hoover Auditorium Brought Historic Speakers to Lakeside." *Port Clinton News Herald,* June 18, 2018. https://www.portclintonnewsherald.com/story/news/2018/06/18/hoover-auditorium-brought-historic-speakers-lakeside/709522002.
Unionville Crescent. "Woman Deep Sea Diver Rivals Feats of Men." April 26, 1935.
U.S. Mint. "The History of U.S. Circulating Coins." https://www.usmint.gov/learn/history/us-circulating-coins?srsltid=AfmBOopvIxqgb5QtdtTDJVEKQzMOfel2tazkaYNDvdjZDx3x0G3qzAPf.
Village of Bratenahl. "Bratenahl's Street Lamplighter." https://bratenahlhistorical.org/index.php/gas-street-lights.
———. "The Cleveland Golf Club and The Country Club." https://bratenahlhistorical.org/index.php/country-club.
———. "First Northern Ohio Airplane Flight Was in Bratenahl." https://bratenahlhistorical.org/index.php/first-flight.
———. "Haskell Homes: Newport Development." https://bratenahlhistorical.org/index.php/haskell-homes.
———. "Samuel L. Mather Jr.: Partner of Pickands Mather & Company." https://bratenahlhistorical.org/index.php/henry-coit-2.
Wachter, Georgann, and Michael Wachter. *Erie Wrecks West.* Corporate Impact, 2001.
Waldameer. "Park History." https://waldameer.com/about/park-history.

Ware, Eugene. "Houseboat History at Erie's Presque Isle State Park." GoErie. May 28, 2020. https://www.goerie.com/story/lifestyle/presque-isle/2020/05/28/houseboat-history-at-erie-s/1083691007.

Washington Herald. "This 'Pen Woman' Follows Marine Salvage Business." April 14, 1921.

Weiser, Becky. "Cranberry Day." Hagan History Center. October 6, 2020. https://www.eriehistory.org/blog/cranberry-day.

Wicinski, Clara. "Glowing Rocks Are Scattered Across Lake Erie's Shoreline." *Morning Journal*, December 31, 2024. https://www.morningjournal.com/2024/12/22/glowing-rocks-are-scattered-across-lake-eries-shoreline.

Williams, John. *A History of the City of Euclid.* Euclid Historical Society, 2003.

Wilmington News-Journal. "A Christmas Story." December 26, 1919.

Windsor Star. "Barrel of Gold Waits Finder in Lake Erie." September 30, 1939.

———. "Capture Lake Erie Monster." June 1, 1934.

———. "Equipment Is Awaited." October 15, 1934.

———. "Plane Seeks Sunken Boat." June 10, 1935.

Wright, Shawn. "Yankees Owner George Steinbrenner Got His Start in Great Lakes Shipping." Crain's Detroit Business. July 14, 2010. https://www.crainsdetroit.com/article/20100714/C03/100719941/yankees-owner-george-steinbrenner-got-his-start-in-great-lakes.

About the Author

Jennifer Boresz Engelking is the author of *Lost Lake Erie*; *Lost Lake County, Ohio*; and *Hidden History of Lake County, Ohio*. She is a Cleveland State University graduate and award-winning and regional Emmy–nominated writer. Jennifer has been published in magazines and newspapers, including *Echoes Magazine*, the *News-Herald* and *Lake Erie Living*. She was a reporter for several years at CBS stations in Toledo and Erie and has written and coproduced historical documentaries that have aired on PBS. She even once played a reporter in the Tony Scott–directed film *Unstoppable*. Jennifer was born, raised and still resides in Lake County, Ohio, near the shores of Lake Erie, where she enjoys exploring nearby beaches, islands and parks with her husband and three children. Her website is www.jenniferboresz.com.